brand new garden

hamlyn

brand new garden

from bare plot to stylish garden in easy steps

joanna smith

First published in Great Britain in 2003 by
Hamlyn, a division of Octopus Publishing Group Ltd
2–4 Heron Quays, London E14 4JP

Distributed in the United States and Canada by
Sterling Publishing Co., Inc.
387 Park Avenue South, New York, NY 10016-8810

ISBN 0 600 60782 8

A CIP catalogue record for this book is available from the British Library

Printed and bound by Toppan in China

10 9 8 7 6 5 4 3 2 1

contents

Introduction 6

1

Where to Start 11

How to analyse and plan your garden from scratch.

- What you've got
- What do you need?
- Choosing your style
- Making a plan
- Basic preparation
- Summary

2

Temporary Measures 25

Simple ways to transform your garden immediately.

- Instant privacy
- Instant access
- Instant colour
- Summary

3

Make the Framework 41

Time to add some permanent features!

- Permanent boundaries
- Patios and terraces
- Entrances, paths and steps
- Lawns
- Vertical features
- Beds and borders
- Garden buildings
- Summary

4

Fill in the Detail 59

Personalize your garden with design features.

- Planting
- Containers
- Water features
- Ornaments and extras
- Seating areas and furniture
- Cooking outside
- Accommodating the kids
- Low-maintenance features
- Summary

5

Put the Plan into Action 79

6 gardens to inspire you to transform your blank plot.

- The relaxing garden
- The romantic garden
- The urban retreat
- The mediterranean courtyard
- The family garden
- The chic roof garden

Index 104
Acknowledgements 106

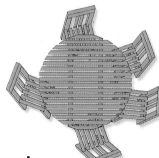

Introduction

When you move into a brand new house, you are likely to be faced with an empty plot outside, an expanse of bare mud staring back at you like a blank canvas. Naturally, the first question for most of us is, what now?

A brand new garden offers a daunting but exciting challenge. There are far fewer constraints than when working with an existing garden, which means more freedom to use your imagination. However, the garden has to be planned in relation to its setting – you may be tempted to create something really crazy because there are no constraints, but you will have to live with the results for years to come, unless you want to start again from scratch.

Your aim is to create a personal space designed to meet the needs of those who are going to use it. It is rather like decorating indoors: there

are three major factors which need to be balanced against each other:

- **the practical aspects of the plot**
- **the proposed functions of the garden**
- **your own personal taste**

in other words, what you have, what you need to have, and what you would like to have.

This book shows you how to follow a five-step approach to creating the perfect garden from an empty plot. It leads you clearly through the whole process, from careful planning, through making the space useable straight away, to ending up with the garden you've always dreamed about.

step 1

is planning and preparation. You need to assess what you've got now and consider how this may affect your plans for the garden. You should then draw up a list of all the features you need to have in the garden, plus all the things you'd like to have and evaluate these lists against practical considerations. The next stage is to combine all these features into an attractive, cohesive plan with a design and style which suits you and your house.

step 2

makes the garden useable straight away. There's no point in having great plans for a wonderful garden if you have to wait five years to use it. There are many cheap and cheerful measures you can take to create an outside space you can enjoy from the outset, somewhere you can sit and relax, cook outside, enjoy some privacy and entertain friends in a colourful setting.

step 3

builds the framework of the garden and can be completed in stages as and when you have the time and money. Many garden features are costly and disruptive to build, so take your time installing the major features, such as patios, walls, pergolas, paths and sheds which will form the backbone of your garden plan.

step 4

adds the details to the garden, the finishing touches which will add a personal touch to your space, such as the plants, furniture, water features and ornaments which really reflect your style and make the garden come to life.

step 5

is about putting the plan into action. Now you know the theory, it's time to create your own garden from scratch. This section in the book shows how the five-step plan works in reality, by taking six sample gardens and showing how they evolve from blank canvas to gorgeous garden.

Some of the most successful gardens look like they haven't been planned at all, but have simply evolved without any intervention. This is usually not true – the appealing sprawl of lavender over a path or the way a weeping willow dips its fingers into a pond often owes as much to gardener's forethought as to nature, so planning is very important.

It is preferable to plan a garden as a whole from the start, with an attractive basic framework with which you will be happy for many years to come. If you plan the long-term features in advance, such as the patio, walls and trees, you won't need to move them later. The smaller details can be changed at a later date but it is important to have a cohesive, balanced framework to hang the garden on and avoid costly mistakes. This book shows you how to tackle this process from the start, from daunting mud patch to your ideal garden in five simple steps.

step 1
Where to Start

- What you've got   12
- What do you need?   14
- Choosing your style   16
- Making a plan   18
- Basic preparation   20
- Summary   22

What you've got

Before you do anything, you need to assess what you already have on your plot, because this will affect your plans for the garden or for particular areas of it. Walk around the plot, taking note of all the features described below. It is a good idea to keep a notebook handy so that you can write down ideas as you look at other people's gardens or see something you like on television.

Rubble

Most builders or developers leave some signs of their presence in the form of rubbish and rubble. You will need to deal with this before you can start to create a garden. Even if the site appears to be clear, dig holes in several places around the plot to make sure the soil is deep enough for cultivation and that there is nothing unexpected lying under the surface. If you are very unlucky, you may find that the fine soil in your plot overlays a tarmac base.

You need to know about this right from the start so that you can make plans to sort it out. For example, large expanses of rubble could be used to form the base of a scree or gravel garden for plants that prefer poor, dry soil, or you could build a terrace over areas that are very badly affected. This would save a lot of time and trouble moving the rubble. If you know about problems like these early on, you can incorporate them into your design.

Soil

Builders often remove the fine, fertile topsoil when they are working and replace it when they have finished. However, some builders sell the valuable topsoil and leave you with subsoil, which is not suitable for growing plants. You need to work out what you've got in different areas of the garden.

Topsoil is dark and crumbly, while subsoil is much paler and coarser. Dig holes in several places to check how much topsoil you've got and how deep it is. This will affect where you position your lawn and flower beds.

You also need to check whether there are any particularly wet or boggy areas of soil, which will affect what you can do in different areas.

Services

Your garden may contain various underground services, such as pipes and cables for gas, electricity and water. Make sure you know where they are so that you can avoid damaging them when you come to create your garden. Try not to devise a layout that requires these services to be moved, because this can be expensive.

Ups and downs

While you are looking around the garden, take note of any sloping ground or changes in level. Most people are inclined to level out a site before they create a garden, but a change in level can make the design more interesting. A slope can be used to create one or more terraces, retaining walls, stepped beds, a watercourse or a rock garden. If you are planning a very formal garden or want a large area of lawn for games you will have to level the ground.

Aspect

Make sure you know which way the garden faces, as this will affect your design. For example, there is no point siting a greenhouse in an area that is shaded by a large tree for much of the day or erecting a tall screen along a boundary where it will cast heavy shade across a large part of the garden. Conversely, you need to know about aspect if you want to create some shade.

The direction of the prevailing wind can be an important factor in some gardens. If it is very strong, you will need to incorporate some sort of wind protection into your design. Also bear in mind that features such as a patio, terrace or herbaceous border are not suited to a windy corner.

high-rise gardens

Many new urban properties have a roof garden or balcony instead of a space at ground level. It is just as daunting to be faced with an undesigned space above the ground as on it.

First, have the roof or balcony surveyed or ask the builder of the house to make sure that its load-bearing capacity is adequate for your needs. Drainage is also important, as rain and any surplus water must drain away without damaging the property. There should be a waterproof surface, which can be topped with duckboards or tiles as long as these are fitted so that they don't damage the waterproofing beneath.

'Large expanses of rubble could be used to form the base of a scree or gravel garden for plants that prefer poor, dry soil'

What do you need?

Before you can begin planning your dream garden, consider what are the important factors that would create your own perfect outdoor space. Consult with the members of your household to answer the big question: what will you use the garden for?

Your needs

List the things you have to have – the practical features that must be incorporated into the design.

Must haves

- driveway
- washing line
- shed or other storage for tools
- dustbins
- windbreak
- compost bins
- greenhouse and/or cold frame
- paths

Your lifestyle

This will have a big impact on the kind of garden that is suitable for you. Do you need a low-upkeep living space, or have you the time to tend a perfect plant-lover's paradise?

Maintenance is one of the most important issues. If your job keeps you away from home all day and leaves you feeling tired in the evening, you will have to create a garden that largely looks after itself and requires only minimal attention. If you have more spare time and are a keen gardener, then go ahead and make the garden you've always wanted, with plenty of beds and borders, a water feature and a vegetable or fruit garden.

If you don't have very much room inside, your garden can provide extra living space. Make the patio or other all-weather surface as generous as possible so that you can use the area for much of the year. Position it so there is plenty of space for sitting and relaxing in both sun and shade, plus room for hobbies and other leisure activities if you need it.

Children and pets also affect the way you use your plot and the type of garden you can make. Pets may need a special space, or you may decide not to include too many delicate features for fear of damage.

'Do you need a low-upkeep living space, or have you the time to tend a plant-lover's paradise?'

Children require play equipment to keep them amused, but their needs will change over the years, so create a garden that can be adapted as they grow.

With small children there are also safety concerns which will affect your design: avoid growing poisonous or spiky plants and put that water feature on hold until they are older.

Your likes and dislikes

When you have decided what you need and how your lifestyle affects the type of garden you can have, start to think about what you want.

What do you want?

- Have you always aspired to a large water feature or are fruit and vegetables your passion?
- Do you want space for plants, or simply somewhere to relax and sip a glass of wine?
- Do you need space for games, or somewhere to cook outside?
- Do you prefer sun or shade when sitting outdoors?

write it all down

Even if you already know exactly what you want, compile a list. Writing down the features you want to include will focus your mind, and you will find you have to compromise between your needs, your lifestyle, and your likes and dislikes.

Be realistic, because maintenance is a major issue. How much spare time do you really have, and how much of it do you want to spend mowing the lawn or tending plants? Budget is also a big consideration. Creating a garden is an expensive business – hard landscaping will be the largest cost, but filling a border with plants can cost more than you'd think.

Choosing your style

Once you have decided what you want in the garden, you need to think about the different materials you can use to create those features and the countless ways of combining them into a design. All this contributes to the garden style.

your natural style

- Are you a formal person or do you prefer informality?

- Do you like a neat and structured effect in a garden or do you prefer exuberant borders with plants spilling out onto the paths?

If you aren't sure, look at your house and furnishings for clues as to what you like. This will tell you if there's a style you need to reflect in your garden: a cottage garden, for instance, would look out of place around a stark modern property.

What affects style?

The style of your garden will be largely dictated by the shape of the plot, its situation and aspect. It's impossible to create a Mediterranean-style garden filled with sun-loving plants in a shady plot overhung with trees, for example. Do you live in the centre of a town or the heart of the country? Concrete and chrome look distinctly odd surrounded by flowering meadows, while a hand-built stone wall would look out of place enclosing a city front garden. The designs that work best are those that reflect their surroundings so that they sit comfortably in their environment and don't jar.

Your taste

Nevertheless, you should always remember that your taste should be the major factor and will be important every time you make a decision about the garden. For example, do you prefer lots of open space or a more divided, secret garden? Do you want symmetrical, formal beds and lawns, or would you feel happier with flowing curves? Do you like bold foliage plants or lots of flowers? Do you prefer the clean lines of large paving slabs or the fussier effect of decorative bricks?

' The designs that work best are those that reflect their surroundings so that they sit comfortably in their environment'

It is a good idea to have an overall style in mind when you make each decision, so that you end up with a garden in which all the features work harmoniously together.

Do you have time?

The style you choose may affect how much time you need to spend maintaining the garden, so think carefully before you make a decision. For example, a formal garden is characterized by neatly clipped lawn edges and rose beds, but both of these features are time consuming to maintain.

However, if you make the style slightly less formal, then you can incorporate features such as a mowing strip around the lawn and plant a selection of flowering shrubs that require less attention than roses will.

Mix and match

If you like both formal and informal garden styles, it is possible to incorporate both into your garden by using them in different places. The garden can be divided into a number of distinct areas using hedges or trellis and each can be planned as a separate entity. Remember that there still needs to be some unifying element, such as the brick or stone you choose.

Features of formal gardens

- symmetry and straight lines
- paths dividing areas into equal segments
- rectangular, square or circular borders
- statuary and ornaments
- geometric, mown lawns
- lots of hard surfaces
- clipped hedges and edgings
- plants arranged in patterns with space between
- symmetrical ponds with fountains

Features of informal gardens

- relaxed look
- flowing shapes
- undulating lawn edges
- curved borders
- natural-looking ponds and waterfalls
- unusual surfaces
- local materials
- mixed borders
- contrasting foliage shapes and sizes
- close planting so that the plants mingle and overspill borders

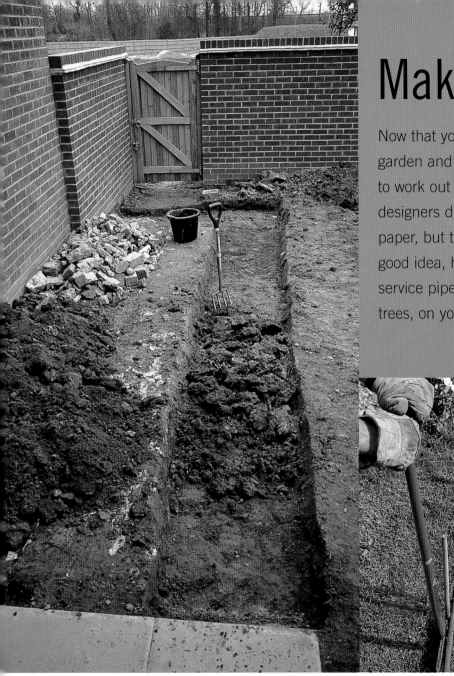

Making a plan

Now that you know what you want to include in the garden and the style you are trying to create, it's time to work out a cohesive plan for the plot. Professional designers draw up detailed scale plans on graph paper, but that is not necessary for everyone. It is a good idea, however, to mark the position of water and service pipes and large features, such as established trees, on your rough plans.

Drawing on paper

Unless your garden is very large or the proposed design is very complicated, a rough sketch is usually enough to make a plan that you can follow to create your garden. Sketch a rough outline of the plot, then, using the list of features you want to include, draw up a garden plan. Repeat the exercise two or three times so that you end up with several plans that incorporate the same features in different ways. Compare these, then select the best plan or the best bits of each.

Drawing on the ground

Alternatively, try the hands-on approach. Use a bundle of bamboo canes, a ball of string and a hosepipe to draw shapes and patterns on the earth. This is simply a full-size plan.

When you have laid out all the features in the garden, view the proposed layout from all angles on the ground, walking around the marked-out pathways and across the proposed lawn to see how it feels, and check the sizes of the features.

It is especially important to view the layout from an upstairs window to get an idea of what it will really look like. This method requires a little imagination, as you will have to pretend that a cane is a mature apple tree or that an area outlined in string is really a border overflowing with flowers and shrubs.

' View the layout from an upstairs window to get an idea of what it will really look like '

a few simple rules

- Avoid awkward shapes in lawns or too many island beds, which will look bitty and make mowing and maintenance difficult.
- Avoid small and fiddly borders, which are difficult to plant.
- Start with a basic layout – the simpler the better – so that you can allow the garden to evolve and add extra features as you wish or need to.
- Make sure some areas are not immediately visible from the house, or there will be little point in venturing further than the patio. Incorporate a few hidden corners, obscured by a trellis or hedge, for visitors to explore.
- Try to break up the plot into smaller areas to give a feeling of space, but don't pack in too much or the garden will feel cluttered.
- Avoid a straight path running from one end of the garden to the other.

Basic preparation

It's important to carry out the messiest, most disruptive work in the garden first so that you don't ruin anything you've put in. The preliminary work usually includes clearing the site, levelling the soil and improving the drainage if necessary. Complete all these operations before you embark on any planting or cultivation. If you concentrate on the basic preparation first, then you can start adding features and creating your garden as time and money allow.

Getting help

Your budget, your level of expertise and the amount of time you have available will determine how much of the work you do yourself. If it's just digging borders and laying a lawn or perhaps an area of gravel, you may feel you can tackle it yourself, especially if you can hire the equipment needed to make the work easier. For heavy levelling or groundwork, however, you will probably want to employ help. In addition, installing a water feature, patio and other features requires some level of experience and skill, and the materials can be expensive, so it often makes sense to seek professional help.

Clearing the site

If the plot is covered in weeds, cut back any woody material to ground level, then dig out the roots by hand if they are not too big. Try, too, to remove bigger stumps and roots as they may harbour honey fungus which will attack new plants. You may need to hire a professional to grind out the stumps for you.

Although many people prefer to avoid them, chemical weedkillers will save a lot of time on large areas that are covered with perennial weeds such as stinging nettles, because the only alternative is to dig them out by hand. In these circumstances, using a rotavator (a mower-like machine that turns over the soil for you) is disastrous because the blades will chop up the roots into small pieces, every bit of which will form a new plant.

Levelling

Think before you expend huge efforts making your plot perfectly level – a slope or change in level is often an appealing feature, which should be exploited and could lead to a more interesting design.

If the plot slopes steeply, you may want to put in some terraces or retaining walls so that you have some flat areas on which to make a lawn or a patio. You may even want to create a slope to add interest to the area.

If the garden slopes towards the house rainwater

may run off towards your property. If this is the case, it may be worth asking a builder to install some drainage to prevent future problems occurring.

If you do decide that you need to carry out serious groundwork, don't forget to remove the topsoil first to prevent it getting mixed up with the subsoil. You will need this fertile layer on top if you want to lay a lawn or grow any plants. The topsoil is darker brown and can be anything from a few centimetres to a metre or more deep. Replace the topsoil only after you have levelled the subsoil.

Rubble

Remove all builder's rubble where you want to make a lawn or borders, because otherwise you may have trouble getting grass or plants established. Collect it up, and keep it if you are going to need hardcore as a base for a patio.

On areas where you are going to build a patio, driveway or path, you could leave the rubble to act as a

'**Think before you expend huge efforts making your plot perfectly level – a slope or change in level is often an appealing feature**'

firm base. Make sure it is well compacted into the ground and does not protrude above the surface.

Drainage

Good drainage is vital for any garden, unless you specifically want to create a boggy area. If pools of water lie on the surface of the soil in wet weather then you have a drainage problem. This can be caused by a number of factors.

high water table If this is the case then you will require pipework to remove the water as your garden will be affected after every downpour.

clay soil This is easy to recognize as it becomes hard when dry, and soft and squidgy when wet. To alleviate the problem, work in plenty of organic matter (such as well-rotted manure or garden compost) or grit to break up the clay.

compacted surface If the surface of your soil appears to have an impermeable cap, fork, dig or rotavate the area to break it up, then work organic matter or fine grit into the soil to stop it happening again.

impenetrable layer If there is a solid layer under the surface, dig down and break it up with a pick or crowbar. It may be a natural band of rock or clay, or – if you are unlucky – builder's

rubble, concrete or tarmac. In a severe case, heavy machinery will be required.

Soil

If you need to bring in some fresh topsoil, leave this until all levelling and groundwork has been done. Only lay topsoil on the areas where you really need it, such as lawns and borders, as it is very expensive and there's no point in having it under surfaces such as patios.

Summary

At the planning stage it is important to work out what you would like in your garden and how it will be used. Make up a wish list and then see how practical it is for your day-to-day life. Mark out where the features of the garden will be and do all the preparatory and heavy work before you begin any planting.

Work out where you will need to lay pipes for water or electricity before you build any permanent structures. It is a good idea to either make plans on paper or to mark out the areas with cane poles. To make sure that you get a proper perspective of your layout, you should view it from an upstairs window.

- It's a good idea to think ahead and lay pipes and cables while your plot is still empty. Look at your garden plan and work out what services you are going to need.

- You may need pipes for an irrigation system or outside tap, perhaps by the shed or greenhouse.

- You may need to lay electrical cables for garden lighting or a pond pump. Whatever you need, now is the time to do it, even if you don't actually create the features for some time.

- You must protect cables with copper or rigid plastic pipes. Mark on the surface where the cables and pipes have been laid, so that when you come to construct the garden you don't damage them. Lay tiles over any cables so that they are protected further.

- Avoid running pipes across proposed borders, where they could be damaged most easily. Wherever possible, lay them along the edge of a path or patio instead.

step 2

Temporary Measures

- Instant privacy 26

- Instant access 30

- Instant colour 34

- Summary 38

Instant privacy

Privacy is one of the most important factors in the creation of a successful garden. Most people want their garden to be a secluded haven, an intimate space in which they can relax without being overlooked by the neighbours or from the road. If there isn't one already in place, put up a suitable boundary as a matter of priority.

Quick and easy screening

If you are planning to have a smart brick wall in the long term or aren't sure what type of garden you will create, install a cheap, temporary boundary to give you some privacy straight away. You can use this as a backing for a slow-growing hedge, which can be removed when the hedge is tall enough to provide shelter and privacy itself.

Trellis makes an attractive and inexpensive instant boundary, especially when it is teamed with fast-growing climbing plants to add colour and more privacy. Many different designs are available, and it can be made even more decorative by the use of woodstain or paint (see pages 28–9) to create a range of vibrant effects. Choose a relatively simple design to keep the cost

down and buy large panels to make it quicker to erect.

Woven panel fencing is probably the best choice for low-cost instant privacy. Although the panels are not very sturdy, they will last for a number of years – at least until you have decided on a permanent boundary solution or your budget allows you to build what you really want. Like trellis, a panel fence can be made much more attractive with a coat of woodstain or paint. You could also cover it with fast-growing climbers or wall pots of flowers for a splash of colour.

Reed screens offer a natural-looking boundary, which should last for up to five years. They are relatively thin and can be tacked straight on to fence posts or trellis panels for support. These screens are versatile enough to be used in urban or rural gardens, formal or informal settings, although they look most at home in country gardens or those with an oriental theme. Don't confuse them with woven hurdles (see pages 42–3), which are much more expensive. These cheaper versions consist simply of a flat layer of thin twigs arranged parallel to each other and stitched together.

Fast-growing climbers

Climbing plants will brighten a plain fence or wall and add privacy almost immediately when trained over trellis. They can be used as a temporary measure to introduce some colour and interest until you decide what you want there in the long term or until the permanent plants you have chosen have time to grow to fill out the space.

Annual climbers give a bright splash of colour in summer, when you will be using the garden most. They grow to full size and flower in a single season, then die off after they have set seed.

Choose from the bold trumpet flowers of morning glory (*Ipomoea tricolor*), which comes in blue, white, red and purple; the unusual purple-and-white flowers of the cup-and-saucer plant (*Cobaea scandens*); or the clear sky-blue flowers of *Convolvulus tricolor*. Canary creeper (*Tropaeolum peregrinum*) is smothered with pretty yellow flowers, while the well-known nasturtium (*T. majus*) bears larger flowers in red, orange or yellow all summer long – make sure you choose a climbing variety. Sweet peas (*Lathyrus odoratus*) have wonderful scented flowers, while runner beans make handsome climbers with scarlet or white blooms and the added bonus of long pods for the kitchen.

A few perennial climbers are also suitable for quick cover. These are herbaceous plants, which die down in winter months but grow up again in spring and summer, putting on a lot of growth in a short time. The golden hop (*Humulus lupulus* 'Aureus'), is one such plant with lovely lime-green foliage, but there are also a few clematis that will work well. These include *Clematis tangutica*, with rounded golden flowers and *C. flammula*, bearing a profusion of scented white flowers, both flowering in late summer. *C. montana* is not herbaceous – the framework of the plant remains through the winter – but it is very fast growing and will soon cover a large area with pink or white flowers in early summer.

> ‘ Most people want their garden to be a private haven, an intimate space in which they can relax ’

going up

Trellis panels add instant height where it is needed and can even top low fences or walls. It makes an attractive feature, adding interest and avoiding vast expanses of plain fencing. Grow colourful climbers on the trellis for extra impact.

Bright boundaries

Whether it's a permanent fixture or a temporary panel fence put up to give you some privacy until your wall is built, a new boundary can look good from the outset. With just a little imagination you can transform an uninspiring expanse of fence into an attractive feature in its own right, which will make a positive contribution to the garden until the plants are able to grow around it to soften the effect.

Woodstain is one of the fastest ways to transform a fence. Modern woodstains are safe and easy to use, cheap to buy, quick to apply and come in a wide spectrum of colours. The shade you choose will have a big impact on the overall look of your garden, making it look brighter or darker, larger or smaller, modern or rustic.

Exterior masonry paint can revitalize a dull expanse of wall, and there is an increasing number of colourful paints available. Choose one to suit your garden style. Alternatively, use a special distressed paint effect to make the wall look old and rustic. This works particularly well on cement or rendered walls.

Use a single colour of paint or woodstain on the whole wall or fence, or you can liven things up and highlight certain features by using two or more colours together.

The range of effects you can create is almost limitless and you can let your imagination run wild and can be as bold or as subtle as you wish.

'The range of effects you can create is almost limitless'

Changing the colour

There are limitless possibilities when choosing a colour for a bright or large garden but remember to choose light colours for small or shady gardens to make them appear brighter. It is best to pick a shade that will enhance the surroundings and complement the tones of other features around it, including the colour of any flowers and foliage you have in the garden.

soft green The classic choice. It will provide a relaxed look that benefits most gardens and sets off plants well.

blue The cool choice. It makes the garden appear larger because the boundary seems to recede, and is a complementary backdrop to the green foliage of your plants.

yellow The adventurous choice. A bright and exotic contrast to planting, it will make your garden come alive, even in winter.

lilac The romantic choice. Bright and fun, it adds colour in winter and blends in with flowers during the summer months.

terracotta The warm choice. Resonant of Tuscan landscapes, it makes a subtle backdrop to a Mediterranean garden. Planting will stand out well against it.

white The minimalist choice. It enhances a feeling of space and simplicity, and looks good in a cottage garden setting. White is calming, yet lively at the same time.

brown The natural choice. Simple and understated it will blend in with any planting and looks good in almost any setting.

wall pots and baskets

It's not only climbing plants that can decorate a wall or fence: consider planting a selection of container plants in wall pots or baskets for an instant vertical display.

There are many styles of pots specially designed for hanging on walls, and windowboxes are also suitable if they are mounted on wall brackets. The size of the containers will depend on the security of the support, but remember that small pots – especially those made from terracotta – will require frequent watering. Make sure that the pots are easily accessible to a watering can or hose, and fix them securely to avoid accidents.

Instant access

The other vital ingredient that allows you to use your garden straight away is a dry, flat surface on which to place a table and chairs. Bare earth and grass are not hardwearing enough and are impractical when the weather has been wet. If you are planning to include a built-in terrace or patio eventually but do not yet have the budget or time, put down a temporary hard surface so that you can make use of your outdoor space in the meantime. This is also the best option if you haven't decided on the materials or style of your permanent patio and want more time to make up your mind.

Put in a patio

All you need is a dry surface to keep you off the earth beneath. It doesn't need to last a long time, so choose a cheap option to avoid wasting money.

It's a good idea to put down the temporary surface where you will eventually have your patio, so that the rest of the garden can be created around it and you can leave it there for as long as you like. It will be an immediate improvement, so can remain while you concentrate on enhancing other areas of garden.

Gravel is a suitable temporary surface for all garden styles, in any location. It blends with both traditional and modern, formal and informal styles. It is also cheaper and easier to lay than paving or setts. There is a wide choice of materials under the general heading of 'gravel', from traditional pea gravel consisting of rounded stones in shades of brown, to sharp-edged stone chips in shades of grey, brown, buff and white.

Bark chips are less versatile than gravel in terms of where they look good, because a bark surface has a definite, woodland feel. It is good for shrub gardens, jungly dells and shady situations, where a natural effect is required.

It is also good for gardens used by children, because it makes a soft and safe surface for play.

Bark chips can be expensive so check the price before you buy. Also make sure that the chips you choose are suitable for creating paths and other surfaces – avoid composted bark, which is used as a mulch and is much softer but not long-lasting.

Softwood decking can be used as a temporary patio in some situations, if the area to be covered is not too large. The timber will be relatively inexpensive if you use softwood rather than hardwood. Even though you are planning a temporary feature, it is worth buying timber that has been pressure-treated with a preservative because softwood can rot quickly in some circumstances. Decking can be treated with a brightly coloured woodstain (see pages 28–9) to add instant colour and interest.

Instant lawn

Remember grass is an instant, temporary surface that is cheap and simple to lay and will transform a patch of bare earth into a usable surface relatively quickly. Also, it will keep an area free of weeds and looking good until you decide what to do with it or have time to plant or create a garden feature. It is easy to remove the turf when you are ready. Growing a lawn from seed is cheaper than laying turf.

Put in paths

A dry route from the garden gate to the house is as important as a dry place to sit out. You need to be able to get about without having to wade through puddles, especially if you are dressed up to go out.

Temporary paths must be practical but cheap. Gravel or bark are the best options. Unless the surface is perfectly level, do not place a line of paving slabs on the grass or earth as you may trip over them.

prepare for permanence

If you intend eventually to build a stone, slab or brick patio, you could prepare the base at this early stage by levelling the site and creating a layer of hardcore. Then place a temporary layer of gravel or bark on top until you have the time or money to lay the stones, slabs or bricks.

' A dry route from the garden gate to the house is as important as a dry place to sit out '

fast food

While you are waiting to build a brick barbecue, why not invest in a portable barbecue? Even a cheap model should last for a good length of time if you store it in a dry place when it is not in use. Cooking outside makes a garden feel like home and offers opportunities for relaxed entertaining, even if your garden is not yet finished.

Creature comforts

It's all very well having a dry surface to sit on, but you also need some furniture and other accessories to make the garden more comfortable and welcoming in the immediate future, especially if you are planning to entertain your family and friends. You may have plans for a solid hardwood table with matching chairs, or a set of sleek wrought-iron loungers with cream cushions, but it could be better to wait until the rest of the garden is complete so that you can match sizes, styles and materials. Buy some cheap temporary furniture as a 'trial run' to check what best meets your needs. Do not purchase garden furniture in late spring or early summer when prices are at their highest – wait for the autumn sales to pick up some real bargains.

tables The cheapest tables are made from slatted wood or plastic. The wooden version is more elegant, but you may not get a large enough table. Plastic furniture is tough and, if you choose green items, unobtrusive. Another relatively inexpensive option is a picnic table with built-in bench seats.

dining chairs Choose chairs to match the table if possible – it is better to go for a proper set, because mismatched items work together only if they are all attractive pieces in their own right. Again, the choice is slatted wood or preformed plastic. There are also fabric chairs at the lower end of the price range, most of which fold up for easy storage. These are either wood-framed director's chairs or chairs with metal-framed seats. Check their strength before buying and avoid seating your heavier guests on the lighter-weight models.

relaxed seating Deckchairs are classic favourites and are usually cheap to buy. They often come in a range of bright colours, both plain

and striped. Metal-framed, stretched-fabric loungers can also be found at low prices, and may be quite sleek and chic. Padded-fabric loungers usually offer more traditional styling and can be picked up cheaply.

benches Most DIY stores offer flat-pack garden benches, either in solid wood or with cast-iron effect legs. Some of these are simple in design, others are more decorative. Place one in a shady area as some-where to sit out of the sun or use alongside a table for outdoor dining.

picnic blankets Don't forget the simple and least expensive alternative of a thick, soft blanket and some cushions from the sitting room. These can be laid on the lawn on a hot summer's day offering a comfortable place to sit at no extra cost.

Instant shade

The problem with new gardens is that they rarely include any large features, so there is little shade, which is important in hot weather because it can be uncomfortable to sit in the sun. You may have long-term plans for a vine-covered pergola or a built-in awning or blind, but a fabric parasol is perfect for the short term. Buy as large a parasol as possible because they rarely cast as much shade as you think. Choose one with a heavy base to prevent it blowing over. You may find you actually keep it for many years for instant shade wherever you want it.

'Do not forget grass as an instant, temporary surface. It is cheap and simple to lay and will transform a patch of bare earth into a usable surface immediately'

Instant colour

Once you have created some privacy and a place to sit and relax in comfort, all you need are a few patches of colour and interest to make the garden an attractive place to be until you put your master plan into action. This doesn't need to cost very much or to be complicated – just a simple container planted with a few colourful annuals will make all the difference. Maximize your efforts where you will notice them most – start near the house and work outwards, concentrating on the access points that you pass by most often, such as the front gate, outside the front door and the patio area.

'**Maximize your efforts where you will notice them most – start near the house and work outwards, concentrating on the access points that you pass by most often**'

Container colour

Containers are ideal for adding instant interest and colour because no soil preparation is involved – simply fill them with potting compost and start planting straight away. Choose a selection of fast-growing plants that will create impact while you are waiting for the permanent garden plants to grow.

Containers can add height and maturity to the

glazed containers come in different shapes and sizes. Most are in plain shades of buff, green or blue, while others have painted or incised patterns. They are often sold in sets of three tubs of different sizes, which are ideal for groupin, and are relatively inexpensive. The plain styles are most versatile and are a subtle alternative to terracotta ones.

All shapes and sizes

containers are available to suit every site and situation, so choose each one carefully according to the use for which it is intended. **tubs** can be placed almost anywhere to add colour and create a focal point. Group for maximum impact. **troughs** are long, low containers. Use them on window ledges, on top of low walls or along paths as a colourful edging. **windowboxes** are ideal for small front gardens, courtyards, roof gardens and balconies. Choose plants that tolerate dry conditions and remember to make provision for watering. **wall pots and hanging baskets** are perfect for livening up plain walls or fences (see page 29). They are especially valuable in small spaces, where they will make a greater contribution to the overall picture. All sorts of plants – both upright and trailing – are suitable, so use your imagination.

emptiest plot and are available in a range of different materials. The following are the cheapest for temporary colour. **plain terracotta pots** are elegant and fit in with many different garden styles. Choose large, frost-proof pots for maximum effect and to reduce the need for frequent watering. Terracotta is the most suitable material for customizing – paint the pots for added colour or to make them fit in with your style. **plastic pots** are practical, tough and inexpensive, but choose carefully because they can look ugly. Plain green plastic tubs are the most sympathetic, or choose terracotta-look plastic, which can be quite realistic. Trailing plants can help to camouflage unattractive pots, or place them behind other, more appealing containers.

top 10 container plants

- Busy lizzie (*Impatiens walleriana*)
- Hosta
- New Zealand flax (*Phormium tenax*)
- Pansy (*Viola* x *wittrockiana*)
- Pelargonium
- Petunia
- Pot marigold (*Calendula officinalis*)
- Runner beans
- Spurge (*Euphorbia characias* subsp. *wulfenii*)
- Yucca

Put in plants

You may want to plant up a border with temporary plants to make the garden look good while you are deciding on a permanent planting scheme or to fill spaces while permanent plants fill out. Some plants are faster growing and have more impact than others.

Annuals

These are a good choice. These are plants that germinate, grow, flower, set seed and die within one year, so they grow fast and produce flowers quickly.

Hardy annuals are a cheap and eye-catching option. The plants are grown from seed, which can simply be sprinkled onto raked soil and will produce a dazzling display of flowers, often within weeks, all for the cost of a packet of seed. They tend not to last long but are excellent for creating a striking patch of colour.

Half-hardy annuals include plants such as petunias and lobelia, which must be sown under protection and cannot be put out in the garden until all risk of frost has passed. Usually it is easier to buy small plants, often sold as 'plugs', from nurseries and garden centres rather than trying to grow them from seeds. Choose plants that are in bud so that you can select the colours you want.

Most annuals are suitable for both containers and borders, but some are fairly large and make a striking display. Try *Cosmos bipinnatus*, which forms huge branched plants up to 1.5m (5ft) tall with large daisy flowers in shades of pink and white.

Bedding plants

'Bedding plant' is a general term used to describe any plant that is suitable for creating a quick, colourful, temporary display in containers or borders. They include annuals and many tender perennials, which grow quickly but do not normally survive outside over winter. Popular tender perennials include osteospermums, *Helichrysum petiolare* and pelargoniums. Some perennials are large and eye-catching, including the castor oil plant (*Ricinus communis*), which grows up to 1.8m (6ft) tall and has enormous, glossy leaves, and many varieties of tobacco plant (*Nicotiana*), especially *N. sylvestris*, which reaches 1.5m (5ft) and has white flowers.

' Some bulbs take a mere matter of weeks from planting to flowering and can add a patch of bold colour to a border. Choose large plants that will really make a show '

decorative extras

It is not only plants that can add colour and interest to a garden. Consider using statues and ornaments made from natural materials to create a feeling of permanence, to add height and to give you something to look at while your plants grow. There are many styles available, and these objects have the added bonus of looking good in winter when many plants will have died back. They are also available in frost-proof resin, which has the advantage of being easy to move but can look cheap if not selected with care. A pile of large pebbles or a piece of driftwood can add maturity and interest to a garden, too. Other decorative features, including lawn edgings, willow obelisks and pots, also add instant impact.

Instant maturity

large specimens Start with a few of these to add immediate height and make the border look as if it has been established for some time. Shrubs, perennials and large bedding plants can all work well and can also be a focal point for your beds.

fill-in Fill the spaces between the large specimens with plenty of smaller plants. Plant in blocks or drifts of the same cultivar to make them look like bigger plants. This also prevents the border from appearing bitty as the drifts will mingle together.

fast-growing climbers Some perennial and annual climbing plants grow very fast – up to 1.8m (6ft) in a season – and are perfect for covering a fence or wall behind a border or growing up an obelisk to add plenty of growth and colour in a short space of time (see pages 26–7).

close planting It is a good idea to arrange plants close together in each bed so that they fill the empty space more quickly. This will also cut down on any weeding because there will be less bare soil available for the weeds to colonize.

bulbs Some bulbs take a mere matter of weeks from planting to flowering and can add a patch of bold colour to a border. Choose large plants that will really make a show, such as lilies, tulips and large alliums. Other bulbs will not come up for some time. You should plan where each of these bulbs will be planted so that you have an interesting and colourful display when they flower.

perennials Some perennials will form large clumps of striking foliage and flowers in one season and can help add instant maturity to a border. The larger perennials include the following: *Crambe cordifolia*, crocosmias, daylilies (*Hemerocallis*), cardoon (*Cynara cardunculus*), angelica, *Macleaya cordata*, *Miscanthus sinensis* and *Rheum palmatum*.

Summary

While you are working out what permanent features you want in your garden, put in temporary measures that are attractive as well as functional. You can easily create instant privacy, colour and access through planting and painting.

A quick and easy way to ensure that you have instant privacy is to put up a boundary. However, building a wall out of brick can be expensive, while a natural hedge will take time to grow. In the meantime, you can erect a fence and grow plants up it as a quick and cheap way of adding a boundary and colour to your garden. You can paint a fence to blend in with its surroundings or to make a bold statement. Then you can choose plants to complement or contrast with the scheme.

- While you are deciding on what boundary would suit your garden, put up trellis or panel fencing to protect your privacy.

- Decide on a colour scheme that suits your personality and your garden. Remember that small or dark gardens will look better with light colours as they will appear lighter and more spacious. If light and size don't come into the equation, let your imagination run wild and choose any shade from a wide variety of specialized outdoor paints.

- Having somewhere to sit out when it is sunny is one of the main benefits of having a garden and a patio or lawn will help you utilize your outdoor space immediately. Remember that you should always make sure that you have somewhere shady to sit. A parasol is ideal until you have put in a more permanent feature.

- Planting will quickly transform a bare patch. Flowers and shrubs will provide colour and large plants will create instant height.

step 3
Make the Framework

- **Permanent boundaries**   42
- **Patios and terraces**   44
- **Entrances, paths and steps**   46
- **Lawns**   48
- **Vertical features**   50
- **Beds and borders**   52
- **Garden buildings**   54
- **Summary**   56

Permanent boundaries

It's now time to begin the most enjoyable and rewarding part of the process – creating the garden itself. It is immensely satisfying to start work on the permanent features and to build up the bones of the garden. As far as the boundary is concerned, most people either put up a plain fence or keep the one that's there. However, there's a lot more you can do with a boundary, and there's no reason why it can't be attractive as well as functional.

' Boundaries have a huge effect on the style of the garden, especially in small spaces where they are much more obvious '

top six hedging plants

- Beech (*Fagus sylvatica*) grows quite quickly and has fresh green, deciduous foliage, but the brown leaves usually remain over winter.
- Yew (*Taxus baccata*) can be neatly clipped to any shape and has evergreen foliage. It is relatively expensive to buy and slower growing than other hedging plants.

- Laurel (*Prunus laurocerasus*) has large, glossy, evergreen leaves and grows fast. It makes a reasonably big hedge but can be kept neat with careful cutting back.
- Box (*Buxus sempervirens*) makes a neat evergreen hedge. It is best for low hedges, but can be grown taller. It is quite slow growing.

- Firethorn (*Pyracantha*) is an evergreen that flowers in spring, and has attractive berries later in the year.
- Hawthorn (*Crataegus monogyna*) makes a pretty, natural hedge. While it is deciduous, privacy is not a problem. Its thorns offer good security.

Style solutions

Boundaries have a huge effect on the style of the garden, especially in small spaces where they are much more obvious. For example, a courtyard garden is defined by its surrounding walls, which really set the style of the space. In the same way, a formal garden would not be a formal garden if it had ranch-style fencing or a picket fence rather than clipped hedges or a wall around it. The boundary really makes a difference.

A boundary should fulfil two main functions: to provide privacy and shelter, and to offer security by keeping intruders out and pets and children in. As long as you bear these two aims in mind, there are many different boundary solutions that are available to suit every possible style of garden.

Boundary choices

Hedges are handsome and can fit into a number of different garden styles, while fences, screens, trellis and walls can be customized to complement your space and style by using different materials and colours. Remember that the boundary needs to be high enough for privacy but not so high that it blocks out light and makes the garden feel smaller and more enclosed. In some areas you may need permission if your boundary is to be over 2m (6ft) high.

hedges make good backdrops to borders by setting off the plants well, although some hedging plants can compete for nutrients and moisture to the detriment of the border specimens. Hedges made from plants such as yew (*Taxus*) take many years to become established, but they are usually long-lived and offer a good return on your investment. Mature hedges can take up a lot of room and are best suited to larger gardens; they also need regular clipping, so avoid them if time is limited. Choose evergreen hedging plants if privacy is vital in your garden throughout the seasons. Many deciduous hedges become bare in winter, which may be an advantage in gardens where privacy is less of an issue, because it reveals the internal structure of the hedge, which is attractive in its own right.

fences are among the quickest and cheapest of boundaries to erect, although they vary greatly in quality and longevity. There are many styles, each offering its own degree of privacy, shelter and particular visual effect. Closeboard and panel fences create a high, solid boundary that is good for instant privacy, but they can be dull unless you make an effort to improve their looks. Picket and post-and-rail fences are very attractive but offer little in the way of privacy. They do make great garden dividers, however. Because they are wooden, fences can be decorated with woodstain or paint to vary the tone and enliven the garden scene (see pages 28–9).

screens made from woven hurdles are good for privacy and create a natural effect, but they can be expensive, especially if particularly well made. Reed and bamboo screens are also attractive but will need to be replaced after a few years (see pages 26–7). Woven hurdles should last well, also.

trellis is popular and there are several different styles and patterns available. It is no good for privacy unless it is covered with evergreen plants, but it is perfect for dividing one area of the garden from another or for extending the height of a wall or fence with a lighter effect (see page 27).

walls are perhaps the ultimate in garden boundaries, offering privacy, shelter from the elements (for both people and plants) as well as looking good. However, remember that walls can be extremely expensive to build. There are many different styles that will create varied effects. Weathered bricks and natural stone are among the most attractive materials, but rendered and painted walls are also handsome in the right setting, and are also significantly cheaper.

top tips for boundaries

- A boundary will form the permanent backdrop to the garden, the borders and other garden features, so bear this in mind when you are choosing it.
- Try to use materials and a style that will blend in well with the house and other garden structures. This is especially important if you are planning to build a wall.
- Boundaries do not have to be restricted to the outer edges of the garden. They also make useful dividers, hiding some areas of the garden from view and adding to the mystery and interest.
- If you are planning a tall fence or wall, talk to your neighbours and check with your local authority, because you may need permission to build one.
- Building a high wall, especially if it requires supporting piers, is a job for a professional.
- Don't forget that you can do much to improve the look of a boundary with the use of woodstain, paint and plants (see pages 28–9), so you could save on the cost of expensive materials.

Patios and terraces

Most garden owners will tell you that much of their outdoor leisure time is spent on the patio, so this feature should be attractive as well as functional to create the perfect environment for relaxing in style. Creating a patio will probably be your biggest expense in the garden, so it is important to get the size, position and materials right first time.

'A patio must be big enough for your purposes, so decide what you want to use it for'

Where?

The most convenient place for a patio is generally next to the house so that you can walk straight out on to a dry surface, offering an extension of your living space. This is ideal if you are planning to eat or cook outside, and it also means that the patio will be close to a power source for outside lights.

However, if the area closest to the house is too shady or exposed you may prefer to site the patio elsewhere. If possible, choose a warm, sunny position because you can always create shade when you need it. You may want to take advantage of a particularly good view of the garden or countryside. A patio ideally needs privacy and seclusion, so think about where you can be overlooked, although you could put up a screen in the form of a trellis, a fence or shrubs. Avoid a site with overhanging trees because it will be cool and dank, the trees will drip long after it has stopped raining, they will drop leaves in the autumn and the roots may affect the paving.

You could have two or more patio areas to offer sunny and shady places to sit – perhaps one family patio and a more private sitting area elsewhere.

How big?

A patio must be big enough for your purposes, so decide what you want to use it for. If it is an extension of your living space, it must be large. If it is just a small seating area or a link between the house and garden, size is not so important. In small gardens, it may be better to pave the whole garden. As a guide, work out the size of the furniture you want to accommodate – perhaps make newspaper templates to lay on the ground. Aim for at least 15sq m (18sq yd) for a family of four.

Selecting a surface

paving slabs are cheap and easy to lay, and there are many styles available. Precast concrete slabs are the most popular, and stone-effect ones are really quite realistic. The patio should be quite unobtrusive so avoid coloured slabs, especially a mixture of different colours, such as pink and yellow. Real stone slabs are expensive, although they look wonderful and set off plants well. They are more difficult to lay because they are not uniformly thick. Paving slabs can be used to create a wide range of effects by laying them in different patterns and using slabs of different sizes and shapes.

bricks and pavers are versatile and ideal for combining with other materials to make patterns and infills. They come in a range of sizes, shapes and colours but are quite fiddly to lay. A large expanse of brick paving may look odd because the units are so small, so stick to small areas. Choose materials to match the house – a red brick patio would be inappropriate with a yellow brick house. Bricks and pavers can be laid in a range of patterns, including herringbone and basketweave.

setts and cobbles create a similar effect to bricks. Setts are small rectangular or square blocks that lend themselves to being laid in patterns. They can look rather severe, so soften the edges with plants. Setts are traditionally made from granite and are hardwearing if expensive; imitation stone setts are now available. Cobbles are rounded so they are more difficult to walk on, but they make attractive infills and patterns in paving or they can be laid in little-used areas.

gravel is cheap and easy to lay. It comes in several different colours and shapes, and blends with most garden styles. Gravel makes an attractive, natural surface that sets off plants well. Lay a weed-suppressing membrane underneath it to prevent the need for weeding. Gravel looks good with plants growing up through it, so cut holes in the membrane for planting. One disadvantage is that it will need to be topped up from time to time.

bark chips make another natural-looking surface, which is easy to lay. They are perfect for jungle gardens and shady areas, creating a woodland feel. There are lots of different products available, some more expensive than others, so choose carefully and consider how long they will last before starting to put them down. As with gravel, lay these materials on top of a weed-suppressing, permeable membrane to cut down on maintenance.

decking is versatile because it can be cut to any shape and is perfect for sloping sites since it can be built up at one end easily. It is also a good choice for uneven ground because it can simply be built over the top with no need for levelling. Decking has a warm, pleasant surface that is comfortable to walk on. You can create different styles by varying the direction of the planks or applying a coloured woodstain, or by incorporating additional features such as a pergola, built-in seats or railings. Use a pressure-treated hardwood for a permanent deck; it will last much longer than softwood (see page 31) and will not need to be treated again.

mixing materials

It can look very effective if you combine a number of materials for a patio, especially when you are covering a large area. This adds interest and breaks up a large expanse of featureless paving. Consider laying lines of bricks in chequerboard patterns between paving slabs, or leave out the odd slab at random and have an area of cobbles instead – there are plenty of possibilities. On the other hand, avoid using too many different materials and too much pattern in small areas, which can make the space look bitty and smaller than it is.

Entrances, paths and steps

The entrance is the first point of contact with a garden, so it is important to make a good impression and set the style for what lies beyond. Paths and steps help to form the structure of the garden, linking different parts and leading the eye to focal points. All three elements have a very practical purpose, but the styles you choose will influence the feel of the whole garden.

A grand entrance

So that it will make a happy transition between the outside world and your garden, an entrance should blend visually with the garden, its surroundings and the boundary into which it is set.

Entrances and gates set the tone of a space as you enter it, so the style should match that of the garden. Where you can see the house through the gate, make sure that the two work together to create a harmonious scene. A gate can be decorative, or it can create privacy, security or safety for children and pets. Make sure yours matches its function and has a secure latch.

As a rule, the simpler the gate the better – understated is preferable. It can be wrought iron or wood, and most styles can be bought ready-made or you could ask a carpenter or blacksmith to make a gate to your own design.

On the way

Paths tend to dictate the route you take as you stroll around the garden, so plan them to take in the best bits and make a leisurely circuit. However, paths between two features – such as the gate and the house, or the house and the washing line – should be direct, so you

' The entrance is the first point of contact with a garden, so it is important to make a good impression '

are not tempted to take shortcuts across a wet lawn or to step over borders.

Up and down

Steps are an essential part of a path on a sloping site and can also be used as design features in level gardens. They should reflect the style of both path and garden, so the choice of materials may be limited.

Ensure the steps are neither too deep nor too shallow, or they will be uncomfortable to walk up and down. Shallower steps tend to slow the pace, so in a garden it is more appropriate to err on this side.

Choosing materials

Paths and steps can be made from any of the materials you can use for patios and terraces (see pages 44–5), and the same criteria dictate their choice.

There are also a few other options: for example, the most solid steps are made from paving slabs or bricks, but they can also be supported on log risers or railway sleepers and have gravel or bark treads. Log sections can be used to make stepping stone paths and are especially suited to areas of bark chipping. They can get slippery when wet, however, so avoid using them in damp areas.

The materials you choose should combine with the patio to create a harmonious overall design, but you can afford to be more adventurous with a path because it is a smaller area. Combining materials, such as paving slabs with bricks, cobbles or attractive tiles makes an effective path. Stepping stone paths are a good way to cross a lawn or an area of gravel without creating too solid a divider. Space them a pace's length apart.

practical pointers

- Gateways, paths and steps should be wide enough to allow easy passage of people, wheelbarrows, lawnmowers and bicycles.
- Avoid grass paths unless you have a large plot. They quickly become worn, are muddy in wet weather and require regular mowing to keep them looking neat.

- Paths must not become slippery in wet weather. Choose materials carefully and use an algicide periodically.
- Steps should be level. Sloping steps are dangerous, especially if the treads slope away from the risers.
- Set stepping stones in lawns so you can mow straight over the top.

Lawns

Grass is the surface most people choose for covering the garden floor where they don't want to make a border or a patio. It provides a natural green backdrop that sets off garden plants to their best advantage. However, grass is not necessarily the low-maintenance surface you may believe it to be. It needs mowing regularly, and if it receives heavy wear you will need to carry out some repairs to keep it looking good. On the other hand, a lawn doesn't have to be perfect – a few weeds won't ruin the overall effect of the garden.

Planning

A lawn will link the larger features in your garden and can influence the overall visual impact. Plan your lawn as a feature in its own right, rather than as infill between other areas of the garden. The shape should be chosen for its own merits rather than just being the space that is left over.

The length, shape and position of the lawn can help to make your garden appear larger or more interesting. For example, if the lawn is wider close to the house and narrower further away, the garden will appear bigger. A lawn that disappears around a border of tall plants also makes the garden appear larger since not all of it is visible at first glance. Curves and circles create a softer look, while rectangular and square lawns are more formal. Try arranging the shape at an angle to the house for a more interesting overall garden design.

Lawns for kids

Grass is great for if you have children because it offers a forgiving play surface that won't hurt too much if they fall on it. Leave a large area for play since physical games always take up more space than you think they will. If you give children an area of their

> **' In areas that get very little wear, it is fun to create a lawn from plants such as creeping thyme or camomile '**

own there is much less risk of damage to your flower beds.

Choose a hardwearing grass seed or turf that contains rye grass and preferably one that is resistant to drought. This will keep the grass looking good and reduce maintenance. Consider laying a stepping stone path across the lawn where it gets most wear, to avoid creating a muddy strip.

In the shade

Avoid laying a lawn in heavy shade where it won't do well. You will be better off with an area of gravel or bark chips instead, or try planting some groundcover such as mind-your-own-business (*Soleirolia*) or ivy (*Hedera*).

It is possible to grow a lush lawn in light shade, but you will have to choose a seed mixture or turf designed for the purpose.

Practicalities

- Avoid fiddly shapes and tight curves, which will be harder to mow.
- Make sure all the grass is accessible with the mower.
- Avoid grass paths, which will become badly worn and muddy every time it rains, and narrow strips of lawn that are less than the width of the mower.
- If there is a well-used route across the grass, lay stepping stones or a solid path to protect the lawn.

- Don't create lots of island beds in the lawn since mowing around them will be very time consuming.
- Avoid lawns in small gardens because they will get too much wear and soon become unsightly.
- Make the lawn as level as possible for easier mowing and to prevent scalping.
- If your time is limited, avoid the need to cut lawn edges by adding a mowing strip (see page 74).

Vertical features

Height is an important element in a garden – if all the features are at ground level a design can look very dull indeed. Pergolas, obelisks, pillars and arches add instant height and interest, allowing you to take advantage of the third dimension when it comes to creating space for more plants. These structures can add real character and style to a garden, but avoid having too many small, fiddly features – one or two larger ones will have more impact.

Pergola privacy

The word pergola used to refer to a covered walkway swathed in climbing plants – nowadays it can mean any structure consisting of horizontal beams supported by uprights. Traditional walkways are useful for leading visitors between one space and another and they create great visual interest. Pergolas that offer shelter alone – often square or rectangular in shape – create lovely dappled shade and an element of privacy, so they are perfect for a patio. A pergola sets the area apart and makes it more intimate, almost like a separate room, and is ideal for creating a dining area outdoors.

Slender supports

Obelisks and pillars are smaller structures that will add height to an area of the garden without taking up much space. They are primarily used as supports for plants, and can even be used in a container on a patio. Willow and rustic twig obelisks are popular and can be used in the centre of a border to add height.

Arched formality

Set into a boundary to mark an entrance or placed over a path to create a division, an arch makes the perfect frame for a focal point or vista. Placing a number of arches over a path leads the visitor on, especially if the arches partially obscure the garden behind.

Choosing materials

wrought iron brings an old-fashioned feel to a space. It is durable and long-lasting but expensive. Plastic-coated metal structures are cheaper and create a similar feel. They usually come in black, white or green finishes but may look worn quickly.

rustic pole pergolas and arches are best suited to rural gardens, and can be made with or without the bark on the poles. They are easily nailed together with only the most basic of joints, so this is the perfect material for creating your own structures at home.

sawn timber looks attractive and can be stained or painted or left with a natural wood finish. Choose hardwood or softwood that has been pressure-treated.

willow is a lightweight material which is suitable for obelisks and arches but it is not really strong enough to use as a support for larger structures. It creates a natural effect, and its pliable nature means it can be used to make curved structures.

bricks can be used to make handsome piers to support the cross-beams of a pergola. They add a classical feel to a garden and are suitable for building a large structure.

Providing for plants

- If you are growing plants over the top of an arch or pergola, make sure that the structure at least 2.4m (8ft) high to allow space for growth.
- If the arch spans a path, set the posts far enough apart to walk between them when they are clothed with plants.
- The sturdiness needed in the structure depends on whether you want to grow plants on it and what sort of plants. A mature wisteria is extremely heavy, whereas a golden hop (*Humulus lupulus* 'Aureus') dies down each winter so the structure will bear only the weight of one season's growth.
- For pergolas that cover a seating area, choose deciduous climbers because they do not cast heavy shade in winter, when what little sunshine you get is usually welcome.
- If the pergola, arch or obelisk is attractive in its own right, don't try to hide it with climbing plants.

' Height is an important element in a garden – if all the features are at ground level it can be very dull indeed '

Beds and borders

The shape and size of a border can have as big an impact on the garden style and design as the plants it contains, so plan carefully and mark it out with a hose or length of string before you start digging. View the planned border from all angles, including an upstairs window, to make sure that it sits happily in the overall scheme. In most settings, curved edges are more sympathetic than straight ones unless you want to create a formal or modern garden.

Where should it be?

sun or shade Borders that are in a sunny position generally have a different style from those in shade. Shade-loving plants are often more subtle, relying on large, handsome foliage and understated, frequently pale flowers, whereas sun-loving plants tend to be more colourful with larger, showier flowers. The effect you want may influence your choice of position.

soil The quality and type of soil often varies around a garden, so you may want to position a border to take advantage of a patch of particularly good soil for growing herbaceous plants, or a damp area to make a bog garden.

plants If, for example, you want to grow leafy ferns and other shade-loving plants, you will need to site the border in shade. If you want a formal rose bed, this will have to be in a sunny position. You may need to avoid a patch of dry, stony ground if you plan to grow moisture-loving plants, or an area of moist clay if a rock garden is your aim.

garden plan The greatest influence on the position of your borders will probably be your overall plan for the garden. It's more likely you'll end up with a space that needs filling and will then choose plants to suit it.

problem areas It is difficult to find plants to grow in deep shade, particularly if the conditions are also dry. Avoid positioning a border under deciduous trees since the falling leaves will rot your plants in winter unless you remove them. A tree will compete with your plants for moisture and nutrients. Also avoid windy or exposed positions since few plants thrive in these conditions.

Raised beds

These are useful design elements because they provide height and can be made from a range of materials to create different styles. Popular choices include bricks, railway sleepers, concrete blocks, natural stone and logs.

Where the garden soil is poor or unsuitable, a raised bed will allow you to grow your choice of plants without the need for heavy

top tips for successful borders

- Very narrow borders will be difficult to plant – the plants always look as if they have been arranged in a straight row.
- Irregular, curvy borders look informal; geometric shapes look formal.

- Plants spill out of narrow beds. This looks good on paths, but will create a problem on lawns.
- Large borders need many plants to fill them. If you can't get free plants from friends, consider the cost

before you start digging.
- Borders should be in proportion with other garden features.
- Avoid narrow strips of border around the edge of the lawn as this design is dull.

'The greatest influence on the position of your borders will probably be your overall plan'

cultivation. One of its greatest advantages is that it can be reached from a sitting position, making it ideal for gardeners who are unable to tend plants at ground level. Remember to make the bed narrow enough for the whole of it to be within easy reach.

Where you choose to site a raised bed will depend on the overall garden scheme, and the plants you are planning to grow in it.

Rocky outcrops

Some plants need special conditions, and alpines, or rock plants, are among them. They are happiest in free-draining, gritty soil, and some prefer to nestle in the crevices between rocks, which offer some protection from excess wet.

The rock gardens of the past – mounds of soil with rocks placed randomly over the surface – were poor re-creations of natural rocky

outcrops. These days, alpines are more likely to be grown in a level but slightly raised rock bed, or in an old sink or trough.

For best results, site a rock bed in an open position in full sun where it will be at least partially protected from rain and winter wet. Place it close to a path or to the house, where the little plants can really be appreciated at close quarters.

improving your soil

The ideal soil is dark brown and crumbly and consists of a mixture of clay, sand and organic matter known as humus. It does not become sticky or waterlogged when wet, nor too dusty when dry. Few plots are blessed with such soil, however, so you will probably need to improve yours before

you plant up a border. This usually involves digging in plenty of organic matter, such as well-rotted manure or garden compost before you begin planting. This will improve both heavy clay and lighter, sandy soils. Clay soils will also benefit from the addition of grit or sharp sand. Well-rotted compost, used as a mulch, will improve the soil.

Garden buildings

Greenhouses, sheds and summerhouses are among the largest and most expensive of garden features, so they need careful thought. Ask yourself what you really need and what you have space to accommodate, then look at your budget. Buildings are often the last major features to be added to the garden, so if you leave a space free, they can be put in later when you have the time and money available.

Growing under glass

A greenhouse will allow you to grow flowers all year round, to cultivate a wide range of vegetables more successfully and out of season, to propagate plants in ideal conditions and to overwinter tender plants. It also offers the only way to control conditions enough to grow specialist plants, such as orchids.

There are many different designs and sizes available.

Decide what you want the greenhouse for and how much you can spend, then choose accordingly. Wooden greenhouses are usually made from cedar, which is handsome and long lasting. It is more expensive than aluminium but worth it if the greenhouse is to be in a prominent position.

A greenhouse must be set on a firm base, because it will be very heavy when glazed. Lay your own concrete footings or buy a style that comes with its own concrete kerb foundations, which are relatively easy to lay.

Cold frames

Resembling a miniature greenhouse, a cold frame is a useful addition to a garden. It can be used for hardening off plants and protecting seedlings and cuttings, so is invaluable to a keen gardener. Some designs are open at the base, so they can simply be placed on a patio; others are more permanent features with brick bases. Position a cold frame close to the greenhouse if you have one or in a sheltered position in full sun.

The garden shed

A shed is primarily for storing tools, garden furniture, lawnmowers and barbecues, but if it is large enough it can double as a workshop. Some are huge, others no more than outside cupboards, so it should be easy to find one to suit your needs. It is wise to select a model slightly larger than you think you need, as extra space is always welcome and you are bound to 'grow into it'. If you want to use it as a workshop, check that the headroom is sufficient.

Sheds can be made from all sorts of materials, including bricks, concrete panels and steel, but they are most often wooden. Brick is probably the most expensive but also the most attractive, although wood can be stained green to make it recede into the garden or in one or more brighter colours to make it stand out. Make sure the wood has been pressure-treated with preservative rather than just dipped or painted.

Some sheds – especially those made from concrete panels – are ugly, so position such a shed out of sight if possible and plan the garden to obscure it from view. Conversely, a handsome brick or decorative wooden shed can take pride of place and will make an attractive support for climbing plants.

A place to relax

A summerhouse is the perfect place for whiling away a lazy afternoon. It is also ideal as an outside dining room and for storing garden furniture. Designs and materials vary, the structures are often made from brick or wood. Summerhouses can be bought off-the-peg, much like sheds, or designed specifically to match your individual requirements.

Site a summerhouse with a good view of the garden or surrounding countryside and preferably where it can be glimpsed from the house. Check whether you need planning permission before you build it, and make sure you have a suitable path from the house so that you can use the summerhouse in bad weather.

A place to play

A playhouse will give the children a place of their own where they can play away from the adults. It is also the perfect place to store play equipment, such as bicycles and footballs. A purpose-made wooden playhouse – or a home-made version constructed from scrap timber – can be decorated with woodstain or paint to make it much more appealing.

Position the playhouse away from the patio area, but not so far away that you can't keep your eye on proceedings.

siting a greenhouse

- Choose a sunny position that is not overhung by trees.
- Make sure it will be sheltered from strong winds.
- A level site will make putting it up easier.
- Make sure there is access to water, and electricity if you want to heat the greenhouse.
- Choose a site on well-drained ground – wet soil takes longer to warm up in spring.

'A greenhouse will allow you to grow flowers all year round'

Summary

By now you will have an idea of what kind of style you want and where the permanent features should go. You can use a wealth of natural and man-made materials for your boundaries, seating areas and paths. But don't forget about how you would like your lawn to look and what kind of borders should surround it.

Pots filled with different flowers or shrubs create a vertical feature on a patio or terrace and, in this case, they flank the pathway to the outdoor living space, leading you through to the table and chairs. A large amount of privacy has been gained by the solid wall and the flowers that have grown up it. The borders have been planted with a consistent colour scheme and the variations of size and colour of the foliage creates interest.

- Beech, yew and laurel are ideal for hedges. They will provide colour and privacy as well as being a natural backdrop to your garden.

- Patios and terraces are best sited near to the house. You don't have to limit yourself to one seating area, you could create a family patio and a more private area elsewhere.

- Gates are not just there to keep children or pets safe, but should be a transition between the garden and the outside world.

- Lawns are the surface that many people choose to cover the majority of their garden. You can either have a formal-looking garden where there are several lawns that are linked or an informal area which is great for children.

- Beds and borders can have a big impact on your garden. Decide on what plants will suit which areas and whether a raised bed or rockery would suit your design. Remember that you may have to work on improving the soil.

step 4
Fill in the Detail

- **Planting**   60

- **Containers**   62

- **Water features**   64

- **Ornaments and extras**   66

- **Seating areas and furniture**   68

- **Cooking outside**   70

- **Accommodating the kids**   72

- **Low-maintenance features**   74

- **Summary**   76

Planting

The best moment of a garden's creation is the planting. Plants make a garden come alive, clothing the hard features with colour, texture, scent and movement, and creating an ever-changing scene. There are innumerable ways to arrange and combine plants, and thousands of different plants are available. It can be difficult to decide what to include, especially if space is limited.

tips for planting borders

- Start by creating a framework or structure with defined boundaries, and use a few large plants, such as shrubs or small trees to form the backbone of the scheme.
- Next add the focal points. These are the eye-catching plants that really stand out and are used in strategic positions around the garden. They tend to be quite large – trees, shrubs or large perennials, often with spiky foliage or especially large leaves. They can also be plants that stand out in terms of colour, and it is best if they are evergreen so that the garden has impact and structure throughout the year.

- Next add the fillers to plant up the spaces in between the structural plants and focal points. These are the perennials, low-growing shrubs and bedding plants that will form the body of the border, and which will add the flowers and foliage.

Planting styles
Plants within a border can be arranged in a number of different ways.
for an informal garden
arrange the plants in random, interlocking drifts so that they mingle together harmoniously with no obvious divisions between the groups and create a naturalistic border.
for a more formal effect
arrange groups of the same plants in larger blocks to form a chunk of colour that is distinct from those around it.
for a really formal or modern feel
arrange the plants in rows or patterns, using large numbers of the same plant rather than a mixture of different plants.

Choosing plants
Select individual plants on the basis of their overall shape, habit, foliage colour and texture, and flowers,

aiming for a range of plants in a border to provide interest. Alternatively, flower and foliage colour can be limited in a scheme, but remember to vary the texture, shape and habit of your plants to compensate.

Aim for a balance of horizontal and vertical elements within the garden. The verticals are the trees, large shrubs and climbing plants; the horizontals are the low-growing shrubs, perennials and annuals that create a carpet beneath. Don't forget your vertical surfaces when it comes to planting. Walls, fences, sheds, trellis and house walls all lend themselves to supporting a few climbers or wall shrubs, which will soften the effect and add colour to the garden.

The best borders, especially in small gardens, are those that contain something that will be of interest right through the year. Consider the seasonal element of your planting to ensure that the garden as a whole offers year-round interest.

Physical conditions

Your choice of plants will also depend on the conditions in your garden. Look at the plants in neighbouring gardens to see what grows well in your area. The following factors will affect which plants are suitable for your garden.

soil type Few plants will thrive in any soil. Most species prefer either moist or dry, alkaline or acid. You can determine the pH (acidity or alkalinity) of your soil with a simple soil-testing kit, and crumble a little between your fingers to decide whether it is moist and heavy or dry and dusty, then choose plants accordingly.

sun or shade As with soil type, plants have their favourite light conditions, whether it's full sun, dappled shade or shade all day long. Depending on which way it faces, each border will probably have different light conditions at different times of day (for example, full sun in the morning, then dappled shade from midday), so

make a note of the progress of the sun through the day.

sheltered or exposed Some plants are better suited than others to withstanding strong winds or frost, so choose carefully if your border is in an exposed position. House and garden walls, especially if they face south or west, offer good shelter for plants and may allow you to grow plants that would otherwise not be hardy.

space Some people forget that a tree or shrub will eventually reach its full height and spread, even though it looks manageable in the pot in the garden centre. Choose plants that will not quickly outgrow the space you have for them. Cutting back a tree or shrub to keep it confined is time consuming and suitable only for certain plants – others look terrible if you remove bits and ruin the shape.

'Look at the plants in neighbouring gardens to see what grows well in your area'

Containers

Containers should form an integral part of the overall garden scheme, rather than being popped in at random. They can be used as part of the garden design to add a focal point, introduce a little height, or soften a plain wall. In courtyard gardens, roof gardens and balconies containers are often the only form of planting, so they really need to be chosen and planted with care.

'In some gardens, such as courtyards, roof gardens and balconies, containers are often the only form of planting'

Selecting a style

There is a vast range of containers available, from highly decorative stone urns to stark, straight-sided metal cylinders and everything in between. Try to tie them in with the style of the garden: for example, use simple terracotta flowerpots for a cottage or country garden, patterned terracotta to create a Mediterranean feel, and lead or stone planters and urns for a classical, more formal theme. Make sure, too, that the plants enhance the style of container. A single architectural specimen will grace a modern, graphic pot, while a decorative painted pot is crying out for clouds of flowers in pastel shades.

terracotta is a cheap, versatile material that looks at home in many settings, from country gardens to formal schemes.

glazed ceramic pots are widely available and come in many different designs. They are inexpensive, and the plainer designs are well suited to most gardens, whatever the style.

stone and cement urns and troughs have classical appeal and are generally quite decorative. Real stone is expensive, but planters made from stone-effect cement or reconstituted stone can look quite realistic.

wood is used to make smart, formal Versailles tubs and windowboxes, which are either painted or left in their natural colour. Wooden half-barrels are also widely available; these are cheap and add a rustic note.

lead is suitable for formal gardens and it is usually formed into troughs or urns. Real lead is prohibitively expensive and very heavy, but there are some realistic imitations available, especially from mail-order suppliers.

galvanized metal creates a sleek, modern feel in a garden. Choose graphic plants, such as grasses and succulents, to complement the style.

plastic containers can be unattractive, so choose with care. It is, however, a light and inexpensive material.

wicker brings a rustic, natural look to the garden and it is mainly used for hanging baskets. It is very attractive but it will only last for only a few years.

Choosing plants

Containers can be planted up with bedding plants, which have to be changed two or three times a year, or with a permanent display of shrubs, small trees or perennials. Bedding displays tend to be more colourful but involve more work. They also often rely too heavily on flowers and not enough on handsome foliage, which has a much longer season.

- Standards and small trees make good architectural subjects. Try cordyline, acers and bay trees (*Laurus nobilis*).
- For a formal effect, use small topiary shapes of clipped box (*Buxus sempervirens*), bay (*Laurus nobilis*), ivy (*Hedera*) or *Lonicera nitida*.
- Hostas and other large-leaved perennials make eye-catching container subjects from spring through to autumn. You could also try rodgersia, ligularia, gunnera or acanthus for an elegant, understated effect.
- Bulbs are great for seasonal displays and also for permanent tubs, where they should come up year after year. Try daffodils (*Narcissus*), tulips and crocuses.
- There are too many suitable bedding plants to list, so take your chance and try whatever catches your eye. If they don't perform well, don't worry – you will be replacing them soon anyway. The advantage of bedding is that you can change the style or colour of the display as the mood takes you, but make sure it still sits comfortably with the surrounding garden.
- Many shrubs also make great container subjects. Try hydrangeas, philadelphus and choisya for flowers, and pyracantha or holly for berries. Shrubs with two seasons of interest, such as witch hazel (*Hamamelis*), with its winter flowers and autumn foliage, are especially good.

creating a display

Containers are especially valuable in difficult situations because they allow plants to thrive where they wouldn't otherwise, particularly on balconies or roof gardens. Try to arrange containers in groups if possible, because they will have more impact, unless you are creating a single, bold focal point. Position them against a plain backdrop, such as a wall or hedge, to show them off to advantage. Two matching pots on either side of a doorway, gate or path really frame the scene, or try positioning a line of pots along a path or on the edge of a flight of steps.

Water features

Even the smallest of gardens can accommodate a water feature, whether it is a natural-looking pond, a small, smart pool or a bubbling fountain. Moving water adds a soothing sound to the garden, and any type of water feature will reflect light and make the space around it seem larger. Water also brings wildlife to the garden, making it an even more fascinating place in which to relax.

Formal or naturalistic?

Whatever type of water feature you choose, it must be in sympathy with the surrounding garden. If the rest of your garden is relatively formal, choose a square or circular pool with a paved edging and perhaps a fountain in the centre. For a more informal plot, go for a natural wildlife pond with gently sloping sides covered by cobbles and planted up with moisture-loving plants. Make the pond as large as you can as it will be easier to keep the water clear, and avoid fiddly bends or narrow sections that will become choked with weed.

Moving water

A gurgling fountain makes a lovely feature for a small garden or a patio area. It will be pleasing to look at and relaxing to listen to.

Easy-to-install kits are widely available and the choice of styles is vast. The fountain can spill into a small bowl or disappear through a layer of cobbles or stones to an underground tank.

Fountains can also be installed in ponds to create a formal feel as well as to oxygenate the water. There is a whole host of pump nozzles that create different jets and patterns of flow.

water plants

Some plants thrive in deep water, some in shallow water, and others simply require moist soil. Most garden ponds can accommodate all three.

- Marginal plants grow at the edges of ponds. They prefer to have their roots in shallow water, so grow them either in the soil around the sides of the pond or in a basket on a shelf.

- Floating plants grow in the soil, or a basket, at the bottom of the pond, and their leaves and flowers float on the water surface. The best known of this group are water lilies (*Nymphaea*).
- Bog plants require reliably moist soil and will thrive in a bog garden. They include hostas, rodgersias, astilbes and rheums.

- Oxygenators, which are available from large garden and aquatic centres, help to keep the water fresh by releasing oxygen and are vital if you want fish in the pond. All parts of the plant grow underwater, though they sometimes flower on the surface. Some grow rapidly, so ask for advice about suitable species for your pond.

' Moving water adds a soothing sound to the garden, and any type of water feature will reflect light and make the space around it seem larger '

If you have a slope or change of level in the garden, you could use it to construct a waterfall. The cascade could flow into a pond at the bottom and a water pump will push it back up to the top. Aim to make the surroundings as natural as possible and make sure they blend in with the rest of the garden.

The right spot
Site a pond in a sunny spot away from overhanging trees, which would fill it with leaves in autumn and upset the balance of the water. Many water plants require sun to thrive, or they become spindly and drawn. If you want a water feature in shade, install a fountain without standing water.

Safety first
Water is potentially lethal for young children, but there are water features that are safe. Any of the bubble fountains that spurt water from a millstone, flowerpot or large boulder are safe, as the holding reservoir is underground. These can be free-standing features or mounted on a wall, and there are plenty of styles to choose from. Standard ponds can be made safe by the addition of a rigid wire grille on the top. The grille must be fixed securely and able to support the weight of a child without bending. Some attractive grilles are now available that actually enhance the appearance of the pond.

Ornaments and extras

Careful positioning of a piece of sculpture or a garden ornament will bring your garden to life. Ornaments add a finishing touch, introduce an all-important element of surprise and reflect your taste and personality in a way no other garden feature can. They can also be used as focal points to lead the eye around the garden and to distract it from the areas that are less pleasing.

Selecting a style

As they are all about enjoyment, ornaments can be eye-catching or subtle, traditional or modern – it's up to you. Your choice will depend largely on your personal taste and the look of your house and garden. In a limited space, an ornament of any size will have an effect out of proportion to its size, so take care that it is not too overpowering. In a large area, however, you'll need something big and bold.

The most obvious choice is a statue, which will look wonderful in a formal setting, even if it is made of reconstituted stone rather than the real thing. However, all sorts of other items can be used as ornaments – just let your imagination take over.

It is better to buy one good piece rather than a selection of smaller ornaments, as it will have much more impact and be noticed by everyone who visits. Aim to be quite dramatic: a number of smaller pieces may simply compete for attention.

statues Usually made from reconstituted stone or cement, statues add instant classical style to a garden. They must be sited carefully or they will look out of place. Place a statue where it can be combined with clipped hedges, stone paving and gravel in a formal layout.

sculptures There are many different styles and forms. Often made from wood, ceramic, clay or bronze, sculptures can be found at craft and garden shows, or can be commissioned direct from the artist. Some pieces are great fun, but try not to mix too many styles.

pots and urns Many terracotta, stone and lead containers are spectacular enough to be classed as garden ornaments. They don't have to be planted, as they are often decorative enough to stand alone. If you do plant them up, try not to detract from the pot itself – use foliage and flowers sparingly so that they enhance the pot rather than hide it.

sundials and birdbaths These are popular ornaments, usually made from cement or reconstituted stone. They make ideal centrepieces for patios in formal settings, or can be set in a border in a more informal scheme.

architectural relics Pieces of handsome stone archway or coping stone, decorative railings or pillars or even old-fashioned chimney pots make good garden ornaments. Use them to enhance formal or classical gardens by placing them subtly where they will be discovered almost accidentally. These pieces are best used to add decorative detail rather than being focal points.

garden implements Old wooden-handled garden forks, galvanized watering cans, wicker baskets or stacks of old terracotta pots make perfect ornaments in country-style gardens. Position them so that they look as if they have been abandoned rather than carefully placed.

natural materials Smooth pieces of driftwood, large handsome rocks, river-washed cobbles and gnarled tree stumps are also decorative in the right setting. Keep an eye open for decorative objects like these when you are out for country walks.

'Careful positioning of a piece of sculpture or a garden ornament will bring your garden to life'

the right position

- An ornament can be used as a central feature in a small courtyard garden or in a specific area of a larger garden.
- Position ornaments so that they look good throughout the year and from all angles.
- Use a statue or sculpture at the junction of two paths to encourage visitors to pause and reflect.
- For maximum impact, stand a sculpture where it can be viewed against a plain backdrop or where it will be attractively framed by foliage.
- Try to position really good pieces where they can be lit artificially in the evening.

Seating areas and furniture

Probably the greatest joy in having a garden is being able to sit out in the open air, surrounded by the scents and sounds of flowers and wildlife. In any garden you should make provision for sitting outside, whether for a leisurely lunch under the shade of a vine-clad pergola or a quick cup of coffee on a bench in the sun.

Choosing furniture

Good-quality garden furniture is an excellent investment, and it should last for many years. Choose at least some furniture that is weatherproof and can stand outside all year, to reduce the need for storage space. You will also be able to pop outside to enjoy a few minutes of clear winter sunshine should it appear.

As with anything you buy for the garden (or house),

make sure the style is right for its surroundings. It is a good idea to choose fairly plain styles in case you decide to make changes to the garden later on.

Wood is the classic choice for a dining set. It is durable and warm to sit on, and there are many handsome designs now available. Buy furniture in a sturdy hardwood, such as teak, so that you do not need to keep treating it with

preservative. It should repay you with years of service. It should repay you with years of service. Be sure to choose furniture which has been made from wood from a renewable source.

Painted metal or cast iron can be surprisingly comfortable. Ornate fretwork furniture is decorative and adds an old-fashioned feel, or choose minimalist styles for a more modern setting.

Dining in style

A dining area should be inviting and intimate. It is a good idea to screen it off from the rest of the garden by using tall plants or trellis screens. Try to include some scented plants close by – climbers such as jasmine (*Jasminum officinale*) over a pergola, for example, or lilies or tobacco plants (*Nicotiana*) in tubs – to perfume the air as you enjoy your meal.

Lighting is also vital if you plan to eat outside in the evenings. Install some subtle electric lighting (make sure cables are installed at an early stage; see pages 18–19) or use candles and flares to create the right atmosphere.

Choose a dining set that is large enough for your purposes. There is nothing worse than cramming guests too close together when they want to relax. A few fold-away chairs will be useful for large parties. Also, you should make sure the furniture is comfortable, as a meal can last for several hours.

creating shade

Shade is much more comfortable than sun in hot weather so make some provision for it, particularly around a dining area.

A pergola clothed with a vine and some scented climbers is the perfect choice and makes the dining area more intimate. Awnings and roll-down blinds allow you to have shade or sun as you prefer, and can look very attractive. Large canvas umbrellas can also be put up and down at will, and can stand over a dining table or be moved around the garden as they are needed. Unbleached cream or green are the colours to choose for understated elegance, and a wooden-framed umbrella will match a wooden table and chairs.

> ' Benches should be compulsory in every garden – there's something rather sociable about sitting side by side and admiring the view '

Relaxing in comfort

loungers are the ultimate in comfort, and come in many different styles and materials. Most have metal frames and plain or cushioned fabric.

Choose a lounger with an adjustable back so that you can get the perfect angle.

wooden steamer chairs were originally used on cruise ships. Their classic design and box cushions create an elegant, formal effect.

The disadvantage to them is that they are heavy to move but the advantage is that they are very comfortable.

deckchairs are cheap and comfortable. They make an excellent standby if you have any unexpected guests and they fold up flat for easy storage. Buy good-quality deckchairs and choose colourful fabric – they aren't designed to be tasteful.

benches should be compulsory in every garden – there's something rather sociable about sitting side by side and admiring the view.

Some benches are neat and will fit into a limited space while others are more stately and make a grand focal points.

In order to make sure that your bench will last, you should always buy a good-quality hardwood or pretty cast iron model.

occasional chairs offer flexibility. It is good to have a few seats or small benches around the garden to offer you a choice of places to sit as the mood takes you and as the sun shines on different parts of the garden.

Cooking outside

Most of us love the idea of being able to cook outside, and a barbecue seems to epitomize what a warm day in the garden means. Outdoor cooking has long been popular in Mediterranean countries but the idea is rapidly spreading to cooler climes as a great way to spend an afternoon or evening in the garden, and the perfect way to entertain.

Choosing a barbecue

First, ask yourself how often you are likely to use the barbecue. Some are cheap and fine for occasional use; others are expensive but well worth the money if you will be using the barbecue frequently.

The next thing to consider is how much space is available, not only on the patio when you are using the barbecue but also for storage in a garage or shed for the rest of the year. Do you really need a large barbecue? Work out how many people you usually cook for and buy a barbecue of a suitable size.

Finally you need to decide if you want a portable or a built-in barbecue. A portable barbecue can be moved around the garden to find the best spot for the weather conditions, but you will have to find somewhere to store it when it is not in use. A built-in barbecue cannot be moved but it can be designed to suit the conditions where it is built. A well-constructed barbecue can be an integral part of the patio area.

brazier This is the basic style, which can be rectangular or circular, and which consists of an open grill on legs or built into a simple trolley. Braziers vary from cheap to much more expensive and better made. Choose a good-quality model or it may rust quickly. Make sure that it has adjustable cooking heights for more controllable heat, and that it is not so low that you have to stoop over it.

hibachi This style is a rectangular cast-iron barbecue on short legs. Hibachis are small but sturdy and are perfect for small families and camping trips or beach barbecues. They are usually fairly inexpensive but will be long lasting.

kettle barbecue This is a circular brazier with a built-in domed lid, designed for grilling and roasting. These barbecues are perfect for cooking large pieces of fish or meat, as they turn into an oven when the lid is in place. You cannot usually adjust the grill height, so they are not so good for basic barbecuing. They use either gas or charcoal.

built-in barbecue It is possible to buy barbecue kits that can be built into a brick or stone surround, or you can make your own from scratch to just about any design. If you barbecue regularly, it is worth constructing an outdoor kitchen with built-in barbecue, storage space and work surfaces that will form part of the overall hard landscaping of the patio area. A chimney will help to funnel the smoke away and make cooking an even more enjoyable experience.

gas barbecue These are usually built into a trolley that combines a small work surface and space to accommodate the gas bottle. Most models have a drip tray to catch fat, so make sure this can be easily removed and cleaned. Lava rocks are used between the gas jets and the grill so that heat is conducted evenly. Some gas barbecues also have a grill and a solid hotplate for griddling.

Barbecue fuels

Charcoal comes in two forms: natural wood charcoal and man-made briquettes. Natural charcoal is easier to light than briquettes, which are much denser. Both are available loose in sacks, or you can buy them in special packages that you put on the grid whole and set light to. These packages are clean and easy to use, and you don't need to use firelighters or kindling.

Wood is less often used for cooking, but can be successful if you know how. It takes longer to use because you have to let it burn down to glowing embers before you can start to cook. The heat is difficult to control once you start cooking, but you can move food closer to, or further away from, the fire. Hardwoods such as cherry, apple, oak and olive are the most successful.

Gas is probably the most convenient of fuels because it is clean, easy to control and hot enough to cook on in around 10 minutes. However, some people think that the food doesn't have quite the same flavour than if it has been cooked over wood or charcoal and it takes all the fun out of lighting a fire. Gas barbecues are more expensive and you have to refill the gas bottle from time to time.

the right place

- Make sure that the barbecue is placed far enough away from your neighbours so that they are not affected by the smoke and smells.
- Do not position it near overhanging foliage or a fence that may catch on fire.
- Keep the barbecue away from the dining area or you will be inundated with smoke while you are trying to eat.
- It should be far enough away from the house to avoid the smoke blowing in, but not so far down the garden that you have to walk a long way with trays of food.
- Keep the barbecue away from strong winds, otherwise the fuel will burn away quickly.
- Never leave the barbecue unattended, especially if you have children or pets.

' Most of us love the idea of being able to cook outside, and a barbecue seems to epitomize what a warm day in the garden means '

Accommodating the kids

Children need to have something to do or space where they can play. However, there's no reason why play equipment cannot be attractive in its own right and integrated properly into the layout of the garden, so that it makes a positive contribution.

The all-important lawn

Have as large an area of lawn as you can accommodate. It is not only vital for physical games, such as ball games, but it also provides a space for make-believe games and somewhere for a tent or a picnic. Choose a tough rye-grass mixture that will withstand heavy wear and that will not look worn in a couple of weeks.

Aim for an uncluttered area where your children can run freely without worrying about kicking the football into a border, falling into a pond or spoiling something. This will also mean that you don't have to watch them constantly. If you plan to have a path across the lawn, make sure it is set at the same level as the grass so that they won't trip over it. Also consider planting two small trees at

one end of the lawn so that they can be used as permanent goal posts.

Play equipment

sand pits are always popular with small children and offer great potential for imaginative play. Free-standing models are available, but it may be more convenient to build a simple sand pit to fit into a spare corner of the patio. The design can be as

straightforward as you like, but make sure it has a secure lid to keep the sand dry and to keep cats away when it is not in use.

climbing frames are also popular – kids love to climb, and it is better to provide them with a safe and sturdy climbing frame than to find them climbing up possibly unsuitable trees. Climbing frames can be simple structures with a few overhead bars or more

complicated affairs with platforms, ladders and rope swings. Buy a ready-made one or make your own, taking care to avoid rough wood or protruding screws, which will catch on clothes or cause cuts.

swings are great favourites with children of all ages. They are available in a range of sizes and styles, from plastic frames with bucket seats for toddlers to much larger, metal-framed

' Aim for an uncluttered area where your children can run freely without worrying about kicking the ball into a border, falling into a pond or spoiling something '

swings with flat seats. Make sure that any swing is securely fixed to the ground, and follow the manufacturer's instructions for assembly and maintenance carefully.

collapsible paddling pools are the best option for gardens in cool climates, because when they are full they take up quite a bit of space but will not be used very often. However, on a hot day a paddling pool is a must. Most have inflatable sides to contain the water, although some are rigid and should last longer.

a playhouse will provide children with a place of their own where they can play at housekeeping or shops, do their homework or read a book away from their parents. Some are attractive to look at and, if carefully placed, will actually enhance the garden (see pages 54–5).

Soft surfaces

No matter how careful they are, children always fall off swings and climbing frames at some point, so it is vital that they have a soft landing. Grass is relatively comfortable to fall on, as are bark chips if you make a good deep layer.

Alternatively, lay a carpet of specially designed play matting under the play equipment. This is available in sheets or interlocking tiles, and can be brightly coloured or black.

Young gardeners

Gardens aren't just about play and games. Most children also enjoy doing a little gardening themselves and gain great pleasure, pride and knowledge from seeing seedlings germinate, sunflowers grow or strawberries ripen, especially if they have helped to make it happen.

If you have room, set aside a little space – even if it's just a few flowerpots – for your child to experiment with growing flowers or edibles. It doesn't matter if the results aren't totally successful: it is the process of trying and learning that is fun. Choose reliable growers: runner beans, marigolds, strawberries, potatoes, nasturtiums, poppies and sunflowers are firm favourites.

Low-maintenance features

It's all very well creating a stunning garden, but you've got to keep it looking that way. No one wants to spend longer than they have to on routine chores, so here are a few ideas for making life easier and cutting down on weeding, mowing and watering. The main rule is to reduce the area of beds and borders and to increase the amount of paving, decking and gravel, which require no upkeep at all.

Easy-mow lawns

Perhaps the most time-consuming element in the garden, at least throughout the growing season, is the lawn. When it is in full growth, a lawn really needs to be mowed once a week, so you might as well make the job as speedy as possible and avoid unnecessary work.

Start by looking at your lawn edges. If they are bare and require trimming every time you mow the lawn, you need to make some changes. Install a mowing strip right round the lawn. This is a line of bricks or paving slabs laid at the same level as the lawn to contain the grass. The mower can simply be passed over the top and you need never cut the edges again.

Another consideration is the shape of the lawn. A lawn without fiddly curves, island beds and lots of obstacles can take a fraction of the time to mow. Simplify the shape as much as possible and avoid having sundials and garden benches on the grass.

Dealing with weeds

The next biggest task in most gardens is weeding, which most people hate. Take heart: there are ways to dissuade the weeds from growing in the first place.

Try to arrange your border plants close together so that little light reaches the soil between them for weeds to grow. Applying a mulch will also prevent light from reaching the soil: each spring add a thick layer of leafmould, well-rotted manure or garden compost. Alternatively, use a material like composted bark, mushroom compost or cocoashell. This will also help to keep the soil in good condition and the garden plants healthy.

A weed-suppressing membrane fulfils the same role but is far more effective; it should be covered with gravel or a mulch to hide it. This will prevent all weeds from emerging and is perfect for use in gravel gardens and underneath shrubs (see page 45).

If weeds do appear in your garden, tackle them little and often. You'll save time in the long run by making sure they never get a foothold.

'The main rule is to reduce the area of beds and borders and to increase the amount of paving, decking and gravel, which require no upkeep at all'

Things to avoid

Some features simply take a lot of time to maintain, so avoid the following unless you are really keen.

- Roses have to be pruned regularly to maintain vigour, and many are susceptible to diseases, so unless you are prepared to put in the hours choose tougher shrubs instead.
- A rock garden can be fiddly to weed, so plan yours with maintenance in mind or leave it out altogether.
- Bedding schemes in borders and containers have to be changed two or three times a year to stay looking good. Use permanent perennial plants instead.
- Fruit and vegetable patches can take up a lot of time if you try to grow too much. Concentrate instead on the really special crops, such as strawberries, fresh peas, courgettes, tomatoes and salad leaves, which are far tastier than those you can buy.

- Fast-growing hedges, such as Leyland cypress (x *Cupressocyparis leylandii*) and laurel (*Prunus laurocerasus*), require trimming two or three times a year to stay in shape. Choose something that grows more slowly, or, if you are really short of time, consider erecting a fence instead.
- Small containers dry out quickly, so they need watering and feeding more frequently than

larger ones. Have two or three bigger pots instead of a several small ones.

Fuss-free plants

Plants that are healthy, growing well and in a position that suits them will be far less trouble than those that are not happy. Choose drought-tolerant plants for a sunny spot to cut down on watering, and shade-loving plants for cooler areas, where they will really thrive in the shade rather than struggle.

Summary

Once you have your main structures in place, it is time to think about what you can do to fill in the detail. Have you always yearned for a fast-running waterfall or do you have a collection of ornaments that will complement and highlight your garden? Now is the time to put your ideas into practice.

Plants should be chosen according to shape, habit, colour of foliage and flowers and texture. Combining these elements will add interest in a border. Plants will also provide scent and movement and will attract wildlife. Bear in mind that no matter how much you may like a particular plant, there is no guarantee that it will flourish in your garden. Take note of what plants your neighbours are growing to find out what will suit your garden.

- Planting creates colour and depth in a garden. Work out whether you would like a formal or informal style and plant accordingly. Remember that your garden's aspect and soil will dictate what can and cannot be grown.

- Water features can be tailor-made for any size of garden. Not only is it soothing, it will attract wildlife to your garden. Make sure that children are safe either by placing a grille over the feature or by ensuring it has an underground resevoir.

- Sculptures and ornaments can be placed strategically around a garden to highlight areas or to add an element of surprise.

- When choosing furniture, pick chairs that are comfortable and place benches around the garden in areas where you want to spend time.

- Play equipment should blend in with its surroundings and there should be an area where children can play without worrying about damaging plants.

step 5
Put the Plan into Action

- **The relaxing garden**   80

- **The romantic garden**   84

- **The urban retreat**   88

- **The mediterranean courtyard**   92

- **The family garden**   96

- **The chic roof garden**   100

step 1
where to start

- Remove any rubble and check the drainage.
- Level the soil if necessary because this garden needs a perfectly flat site.
- Compact the soil and add a base of hardcore.

step 2
temporary measures

- Lay gravel over the whole garden. It will form a firm, dry surface until you have the money and/or time to lay the paving at the far end of the garden.
- If there is no boundary, put up a cheap panel fence for instant privacy.
- Buy an inexpensive table and chairs so that you can use the garden immediately.
- Buy a selection of tubs and containers and arrange them in groups. Choose ones that will last for years and plant bedding plants for instant colour, until you have time to choose permanent plants.
- Buy a simple portable barbecue and a few cheap deckchairs and start enjoying yourself.

❶ Gravel forms a firm, dry surface for the whole garden

❷ Inexpensive panel fence makes a temporary boundary

❸ Cheap plastic table and chairs allow the garden to be used straight away

❹ Containers in durable materials planted with temporary bedding for instant colour

❺ Containers arranged in groups for more impact

❻ Inexpensive portable barbecue and a few cheap deckchairs create an instant eating area

The relaxing garden

This haven is for people who want to relax in privacy. It is designed for leisurely barbecues, sunbathing to the sound of a gurgling fountain and dozing in the shade on a hot afternoon.

① Brick wall offers privacy and makes a handsome feature

② Paving makes a more permanent surface

③ Gravel acts as a contrast to the paving

④ Built-in barbecue with work surface and storage space

⑤ Raised herb bed positioned conveniently close to the barbecue

step 3
make the framework

- Replace the fence with an attractive brick wall around the garden. It will last for many years, offering privacy and shelter.
- When your budget allows, lay paving over half the garden for a permanent, low-maintenance surface. Break up the edge of the paving with a few randomly placed slabs for a softer effect.
- Make a built-in brick barbecue with work surfaces, storage space and a raised brick herb bed for the ultimate in alfresco cooking.
- Build a wooden pergola in one corner of the garden to make a shady retreat. Take into consideration the path of the sun to ensure it will shade the area beneath it.

In progress

scale

1m (3ft)

Checklist

▪ Easy care ▪ Few plants ▪ Great for entertaining ▪ All-weather surface
▪ Ideal for busy people and non-gardeners

step 4
fill in the detail

- Install a fountain to provide a gently gurgling sound to help you relax.
- Buy a comfortable bench to fit under the pergola, so that you have somewhere to sit in hot weather.
- Plant climbers over the pergola to create dappled shade.
- Buy a sturdy table and chairs for the patio. Hardwood is handsome and should last for many years.
- Plant up the tubs with a range of shrubs and perennials that will offer year-round colour for many years with the minimum of attention. Plant a climber in one of the tubs to train up the garden wall to soften the effect.

'There is little to do in the way of gardening – it's all about enjoyment'

In full glory

❶ Wooden pergola with climbing plants

❷ Garden bench under the shade of the pergola

❸ Containers with mature shrubs and perennials for year-round interest

❹ Climbing plants on the wall soften the effect of the bricks

❺ Gravel for low-maintenance groundcover

❻ Built-in barbecue with work surface and storage space

❼ Raised herb bed positioned close to the barbecue

❽ Wooden table and chairs made from teak and built to last

❾ Brick wall surrounds the whole garden, good for privacy and shelter

❿ Natural stone-effect paving makes a generous patio

⓫ Fountain water feature – the gentle gurgling adds to the relaxed feel of the garden

scale

1m (3ft)

step 1
where to start

- Remove any rubble from the site and check the drainage.
- Level the soil if necessary, especially around the top, formal part of the garden.
- Draw a plan of the shape of your garden, using the illustrations here as a guide.

step 2
temporary measures

- Put up a sturdy closeboard fence, if there isn't one there already.
- If you don't have the budget to build the brick terrace straight away, make a hard area from gravel or softwood decking so that you can sit out in the meantime. Both are cheap and easy to lay.
- Plant up a few containers of colourful plants to make the garden attractive from the outset.
- Buy a cheap wooden table and chairs or a small garden bench for immediate use, unless you can find ornate table and chairs straight away.

❶ Gravel forms a dry surface at the top of the garden for sitting out

❷ Panel fence makes a practical boundary

❸ Cheap wooden table and chairs allow the garden to be used straight away

❹ A few cheap containers add instant colour to the garden

❺ Hedge has been planted

❻ Three apple trees will eventually form the orchard

❼ Rest of the garden has been grassed so it can be used as an outside space straight away

The romantic garden

This has a formal structure but is overflowing with flowers to soften the effect. It is perfect for keen gardeners who want an old-fashioned environment away from the modern world.

1 Fence stained green as a sympathetic backdrop

2 Attractive brick terrace makes a more permanent surface

3 Herbaceous borders have been dug and planted

4 Box plants will grow to form a neat edging

5 Hedge is filling out

6 Tree seat offers a private sanctuary in the orchard

step 3
make the framework

- Stain the fence green to make a sympathetic backdrop for the plants.
- Construct a brick terrace with the bricks laid in an attractive pattern. Make sure the bricks are weatherproof.
- Grass over the rest of the garden to establish the lawn areas and prevent weeds from growing on the border areas.
- Plant the *Rosa rugosa* hedging plants to divide the garden. Get these in early on so that they can start to grow. Cut out a strip of turf so that the grass does not compete with the hedge.
- Plant the box (*Buxus sempervirens*) edging in the same way. Leave the borders grassed over for now.
- Plant the apple trees at the end of the garden to give them a head start.

In progress

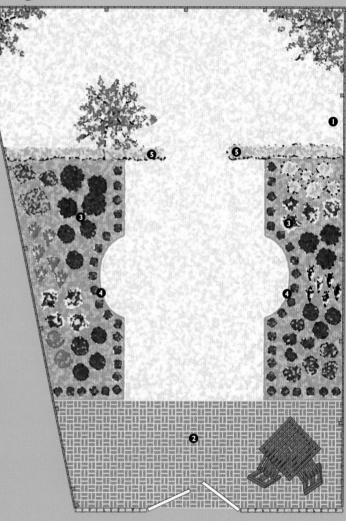

scale

1m (3ft)

checklist

▪ Moderate care ▪ Scope for lots of plants ▪ Pretty, traditional feel

▪ Formal design for most of the garden ▪ Informal orchard area

step 4
fill in the detail

- Measure out and lay the brick path down the centre of the garden, with the brick circle in the middle.
- Add the sundial as a centrepiece.
- Put up three metal arches as supports for climbing roses. Space them evenly, to create a rhythm down the garden.
- Remove the turf, cultivate the soil and plant up the herbaceous borders.
- Make the tree seat around one of the apple trees in the orchard.
- Position the urn at the bottom of the garden to act as a focal point.
- If you haven't already done so, buy an ornate table and chairs to reflect the feel of the garden. White-painted cast iron is a good choice.
- Install a small garden shed or garden store in a corner of the terrace.

'If you are a romantic at heart, this is the garden for you'

In full glory

❶ Tree seat makes a private, shady retreat

Apple trees create an informal orchard area

❷ Grass is allowed to grow longer in the orchard, to reduce maintenance and make it more informal

❸ Urn forms a focal point from the patio

❹ Flowering hedge divides the garden

❺ Three ornate metal arches swathed in scented roses

❻ Herbaceous borders filled with flowers in summer

❼ Box edging makes a neat finish and accentuates the formality and shape of the borders

❽ Attractive brick path cuts straight down the centre of the garden

❾ Sundial positioned on a central circle of bricks

❿ Old-fashioned bricks create a generous terrace

⓫ Decorative cast-iron furniture continues the old-fashioned theme

⓬ Small shed or garden store for handy storage

⓭ Green closeboard fence offers privacy and a pleasant backdrop

scale

1m (3ft)

In the beginning

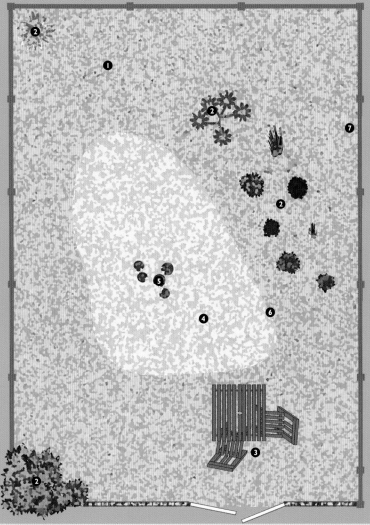

step 1
where to start
- Remove any rubble from the site.
- Mark out the area and excavate the pond, leaving the sides with shallow slopes.

step 2
temporary measures
- Put up a sturdy panel fence if there isn't already a boundary.
- Lay weed-suppressing membrane under the path areas, then cover the whole garden – except the pond – with a thick layer mulch of cocoashell.
- Buy a wooden table and chairs or a small garden bench for immediate use.

❶ Cocoashell mulch covers the whole garden, offering a dry, comfortable surface

❷ Larger trees and shrubs have been planted to give them time to become established

❸ Basic table and chairs can be used straight away

❹ Pond has been excavated, lined and filled up

❺ Water lily has been planted so that it can start to grow

❻ Cocoashell covers the edges of the liner around the pond

❼ Panel fence offers instant privacy

The urban retreat

The pressures of urban life are forgotten in this leafy jungle glade with its cool expanse of water. It offers an environment for relaxing beneath the shady canopy above.

① Pond edged with cobbles to make a natural surround

② Shed for storage space

③ Decking creates a raised seating area overlooking the pond

④ More shrubs added to complete the framework for the planting

⑤ Bamboo plants form a secret glade and create privacy from neighbours

step 3
make the framework

• Line the pond with a thick butyl liner and fill it with water. Plant the water lily (*Nymphaea*) in the pond.

• Plant the larger shrubs and trees to allow them to become established. Choose architectural plants, such as cordylines, trachycarpus, banana palms (*Musa*), aralias, camellias and rhus.

• Build the main square of decking closest to the house. If necessary, the boardwalk and stepping stone platforms can wait until budget allows.

• Erect a small shed in the corner of the garden.

• Edge the pond with large cobbles to create a natural 'beach' all round.

In progress

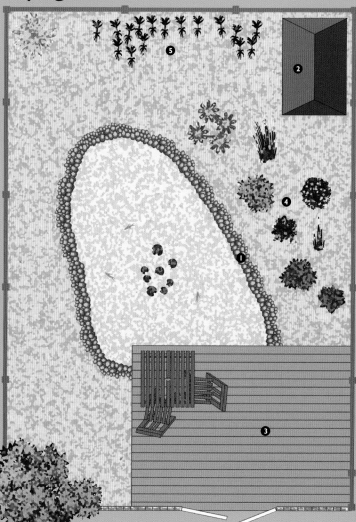

scale

1m (3ft)

checklist

▪ Moderate care ▪ Foliage-lover's paradise ▪ Large, natural pond ▪ Shady, jungle effect
▪ Great for wildlife ▪ Offers privacy from neighbours

fill in the detail

- Build compost bins close to the shed.
- Add the boardwalk and stepping stone decking platforms, if you haven't already done so.
- Stain all the decking and the shed in a shade of blue-green.
- Plant the edges of the pond with moisture-loving plants such as gunneras, irises, rheums and ligularias.
- Fill out the planting areas with more foliage plants, such as hostas, bamboos, phormiums, ferns, fatsias and heucheras.
- Buy a small table and chairs for the deck and a garden bench, if you haven't already.
- Plant some climbers around the edges of the garden to clothe the fences with exuberant foliage.

'This is a shady, verdant oasis, far away from the cares of the world'

In full glory

❶ **Climbing plants clothe the plain wooden fence**

❷ **Stand of bamboo creates a private space**

❸ **Wooden bench nestles secretly in the bamboo glade, offering a place for quiet contemplation**

❹ **Palms and other architectural plants form the backbone of the planting**

❺ **Shed stained blue-green**

❻ **Compost bins allow kitchen and garden waste to be recycled**

❼ **Low-level foliage and large-leaved plants create a jungle feel**

❽ **Large natural pond attracts wildlife**

❾ **Cobbles make a sympathetic edging to the pond**

❿ **Water plants soften the effect**

⓫ **Decking platforms make stepping stones across the water**

⓬ **Boardwalk offers a dry, all-weather platform**

⓭ **Decking seating area stained blue-green**

⓮ **Cocoashell mulch makes a soft and comfortable surface**

⓯ **Weed-suppressing membrane underlies the cocoashell in the path areas**

scale

1m (3ft)

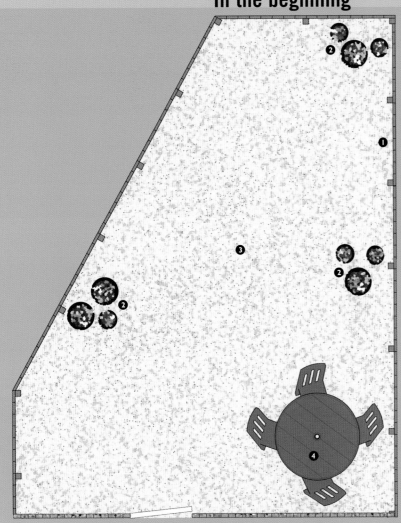

step 1
where to start

- Remove any particularly large pieces of rubble or builder's rubbish from the garden.
- Level the site and mark out where the gravel will be.
- Remove all the rubble from the gravel area. This can be spread onto the paved areas and compacted into the soil, to form a hard base for the paving.

step 2
temporary measures

- Put up an inexpensive panel fence if there isn't already a boundary.
- Cover the whole garden with a layer of gravel to create a dry surface for immediate use.
- Buy a cheap table and chairs if you can't afford a sturdy wooden table and benches straight away.
- Buy some simple terracotta pots and plant with bedding for immediate colour.

❶ Cheap panel fence for instant privacy

❷ Terracotta pots filled with bedding plants for immediate colour

❸ Gravel covers the whole garden to form a dry surface

❹ Plastic table and chairs allow the garden to be used straight away

The mediterranean courtyard

A small plot is transformed into an elegant, all-weather courtyard that is perfect for leisurely meals or lazy afternoons in the shade of the vine-clad pergola.

❶ Flagstones form the patio area

❷ Row of lavender plants will grow to form a hedge

❸ Other shrubs and perennials have been planted

❹ Three cypress trees will define the edge of the path

step 3
make the framework

- Sweep back the gravel from the area to be planted and enrich the soil as necessary.
- Plant a row of lavenders (*Lavandula*) down one side to form a hedge.
- Plant three columnar cypress trees (*Cupressus sempervirens*) in a line down the opposite side.
- Plant a range of small and medium-sized shrubs and sun-loving perennials in the gravel area, then replace the gravel around the plants.
- When your time or budget allows, lay the flagstones on the rest of the site. If you can't afford to do it all at once, lay the patio area first and add the paths down the sides of the garden and the paved area at the end at a later date.
- Add a brick edging in a contrasting colour to give definition to the shape of the paving.
- Build a simple block wall around the garden and render it with rough cement for a rustic look.
- Erect a rustic pergola at the end of the garden, with a covered walkway down the path at the side.

scale

1m (3ft)

checklist

▪ Easy care ▪ Suits a small, sunny courtyard ▪ Good for entertaining
▪ Scope for quite a few plants ▪ Formal structure ▪ Soft, scented planting

fill in the detail

- Paint the wall with exterior masonry paint in a sympathetic colour, such as terracotta-pink.
- Grow a grapevine over the pergola to create shade.
- Plant up the containers with Mediterranean plants, such as oleander, pelargoniums and white lilies.
- Buy a wooden bench to place under the pergola in the shady seating area.
- Buy a large wooden table with two bench seats for leisurely meals outside.

'Soft colours and scented plants evoke a feeling of sunny Mediterranean skies'

In full glory

1. Rustic wooden pergola forms a covered walkway
2. Lavender hedge edges the path
3. Large terracotta tub planted with oleander
4. Rendered walls painted in a soft terracotta-pink
5. Large flagstones pave most of the garden, creating an all-weather surface
6. Generous wooden table and benches for eating alfresco
7. Potted red pelargoniums add a touch of sunshine
8. Tubs with scented white lilies
9. Scented, sun-loving plants grow in the gravel
10. Brick edging adds definition
11. Columnar cypress trees add a Mediterranean touch
12. Wooden pergola covered with a grapevine creates a shady sitting area
13. Rustic wooden bench

scale

1m (3ft)

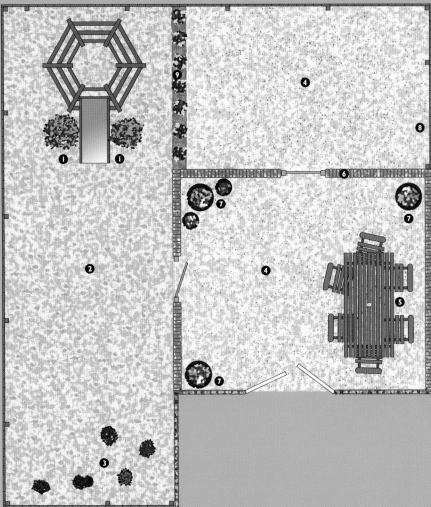

step 1
where to start

- Remove any rubble or builder's rubbish from the garden. Save any hardcore to form a base for the patio.
- Level the patio area.
- Improve the soil in the secret garden and lawn area, if necessary.

step 2
temporary measures

- Erect a panel fence around the whole garden if there isn't already a boundary.
- Mark out the different areas of the garden and lay lawn over the whole of the play area.
- Lay gravel in the secret garden and patio area to form an instant all-weather surface.
- Buy a large wooden table and chairs for the patio area.
- Plant up a few cheap tubs with bedding plants to brighten up the patio area.

❶ Two small trees planted as goal posts

❷ Grass covers the whole play area

❸ A few tough shrubs have been planted to allow time for them to become established

❹ Gravel covers the secret garden and patio area

❺ Large table and chairs allow the patio area to be used immediately

❻ Brick wall encloses the patio area

❼ A few cheap tubs with bedding plants create instant colour and interest

❽ Panel fence offers privacy straight away

❾ Hedge planted early on to allow time for it to grow

The family garden

This design accommodates the needs of a growing family with ample space for eating together and a play area for children. There is even a secret area where adults can enjoy a few moments of peace.

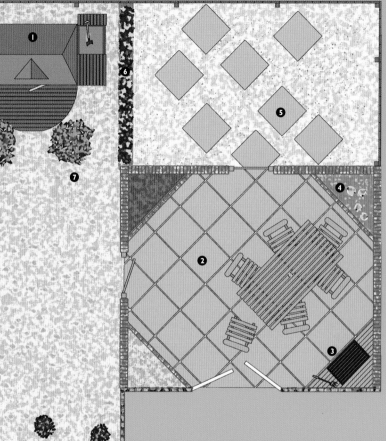

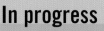

❶ Wooden playhouse with a deck and sand pit offers lots of play opportunities

❷ Patio area completed first to improve the view from the house and allow the garden to be used more

❸ Barbecue for family meals outside

❹ Rigid mesh cover makes the pond safe

❺ A few spare slabs break up the gravel in the secret garden

❻ Hedge beginning to fill out

❼ Trees growing larger

❽ Shrubs getting bigger

step 3
make the framework

- Build a brick wall around the patio to enclose it. Hang gates across the two access points.
- Plant a row of evergreen shrubs to form a hedge between the play area and the secret garden.
- Plant two small trees, such as silver birches (*Betula pendula*), in the play area for goal posts and a few tough shrubs at one end of the play area.
- Lay a slab patio, leaving the four corners free. Install a pond, a built-in barbecue, a small border and an area for found objects in the four corners.
- Lay a few slabs as stepping stones in the secret garden, to break up the gravel and add interest.
- Build a playhouse with a deck and attached sand pit in the play area and lay bark chips at one end of the play area and add a sturdy climbing frame.
- Lay stepping stone paths in the play area to prevent the grass becoming worn. Set the stones below the lawn's surface so that they are easy to mow over.
- Install two small flower beds in the play area to exercise those little green fingers.

checklist

■ Moderate care ■ Enclosed patio area for safe toddler play ■ Plenty of space for barbecues and family meals
■ Large play area for older children ■ Secret garden for an adult escape

scale

1m (3ft)

fill in the detail

- Stain the table and chairs and the barbecue surround in a matching woodstain.
- Plant up the small patio border with plants that offer interesting textures and scents. Choose tough varieties that will cope with being pulled about.
- Plant a few water plants in the pond to attract wildlife.
- Collect interesting objects for the other corner of the patio. Nature walks offer great opportunities.
- Buy a simple wooden bench for the secret garden.
- Plant a selection of low-growing shrubs and perennials in the gravel in the secret garden, and add a few climbers on the fence.
- Stain the playhouse, deck and sandpit in bright colours.
- Get the children to plant up their flower beds. Choose easy-grow annuals or straightforward vegetables.

'This imaginative, child-friendly garden offers something for all the family'

In full glory

❶ Wooden playhouse for relaxation and storage, stained lilac

❷ Wooden deck with cushions for relaxation

❸ Two small trees form goal posts

❹ Stepping stone path set below the level of the lawn

❺ Brick edging to contain bark chips

❻ Small borders for kids to grow simple vegetables or flowers

❼ Wooden climbing frame with swing

❽ Bark chips create a dry surface and soft landing

❾ Resilient shrubs offer hiding places and somewhere to build secret dens

❿ Exploration area for found objects such as stones, pebbles, driftwood and feathers

⓫ Small bed for plants with interesting textures and scented foliage, for feeling and smelling

⓬ Gates to enclose toddlers

⓭ Large slabs form a generous patio

⓮ Barbecue built into a decking work surface, with storage underneath

⓯ Wooden table and chairs stained green

⓰ Brick edging

⓱ Small pond with rigid mesh cover for safety attracts wildlife

⓲ Waist-high brick wall encloses patio

⓳ Slabs laid randomly in the gravel

⓴ Colourful climbers clothe the fence

㉑ Wooden bench for valuable moments alone

㉒ Sturdy panel fence encloses the whole garden

㉓ Gravel with small shrubs and perennials planted in it

㉔ Secret garden for parents

㉕ Evergreen hedge to divide the play area from the secret garden

㉖ Sandpit with a decking lid in two halves for easy removal

scale

1m (3ft)

In the beginning

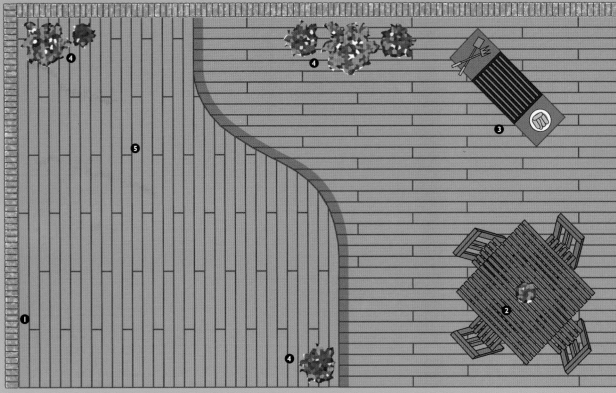

step 1
where to start
- Make sure that the roof covering is waterproof and that the surrounding wall is secure.
- Ask a surveyor to check the load-bearing capacity of the roof before you build.

step 2
temporary measures
- Paint the wall white to add instant brightness.
- Get a simple table and chairs until you can afford to buy the hand-made furniture.
- If you are not having the built-in barbecue installed straight away, buy a portable one.
- Fill a few containers with bedding plants.

❶ White-painted walls enhance the colour scheme and reflect light

❷ Basic wooden table and chairs act as a temporary measure

❸ Inexpensive portable trolley barbecue allows the fun to start straight away

❹ A few simple containers planted up with white bedding add some decoration

❺ Decking overlays the waterproof roof covering

The chic roof garden

This small, contemporary roof garden is the perfect space for relaxing in and for entertaining outside. The minimalist layout maintains a feeling of space and could also be recreated in a small courtyard garden or basement space.

In progress

step 3
make the framework

- Lay the decking over the roof, taking care not to damage the waterproof covering. Lay it on two levels for added interest.
- Construct the bench seating with hammered steel tops. You may be able to incorporate storage space in the seats.
- Install the gas barbecue in a stainless steel work surface, with storage cupboards underneath.
- Construct the wooden raised beds.

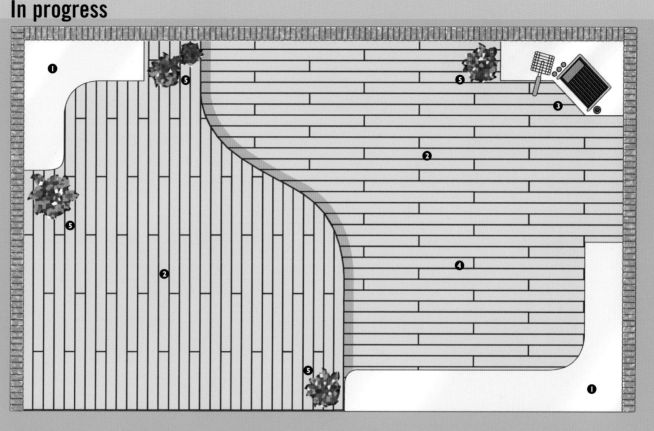

❶ Steel-topped built-in seating offers plenty of space for entertaining and sunbathing

❷ Decking stained duck-egg blue to create a colour theme

❸ Built-in gas barbecue offers great scope for outside meals

❹ Table and chairs still serve their purpose

❺ Temporary containers have been moved to fit the layout

checklist

▪ Easy care ▪ Chic, contemporary design ▪ Perfect for entertaining outside
▪ A few easy edibles make the garden productive ▪ State-of-the-art cooking area

scale

1m (3ft)

step 4
fill in the detail

- Stain the decking and raised beds with duck-egg blue woodstain.
- Buy a hand-made hammered steel table and two ornate, curly steel chairs.
- Buy or make cushions to fit the seats.
- Fill one of the raised beds with topsoil and plant or sow a selection of salad leaves and herbs in it.
- Plant up the raised beds with bronze carex, blue cerinthe and silver artemisia for an eye-catching scheme. The colours can be changed whenever you want to create a different look.
- Plant a bronze phormium in a straight-sided, galvanized tub.
- Arrange a line of tubs, equally spaced, against the step to highlight the curved shape. Plant with runner beans supported on metal spiral poles for added decorative interest.

❶ White-painted wall
❷ Large bronze phormium in a galvanized tub
❸ Decking stained blue, with the planks laid horizontally
❹ Galvanized tubs with runner beans trained up metal spiral supports
❺ Built-in steel-topped seating
❻ Large cushions
❼ Steel table
❽ Ornate steel chairs
❾ Built-in wooden planter stained blue, with bronze, blue and silver planting
❿ Large gas barbecue set into a stainless steel surround with storage space underneath
⓫ Built-in wooden planter with salad vegetables and herbs
⓬ Decking planks laid vertically
⓭ Change in level – a step up to the seating area and barbecue

'The perfect space for a bachelor or a professional couple with a hectic lifestyle'

scale

1m (3ft)

In full glory

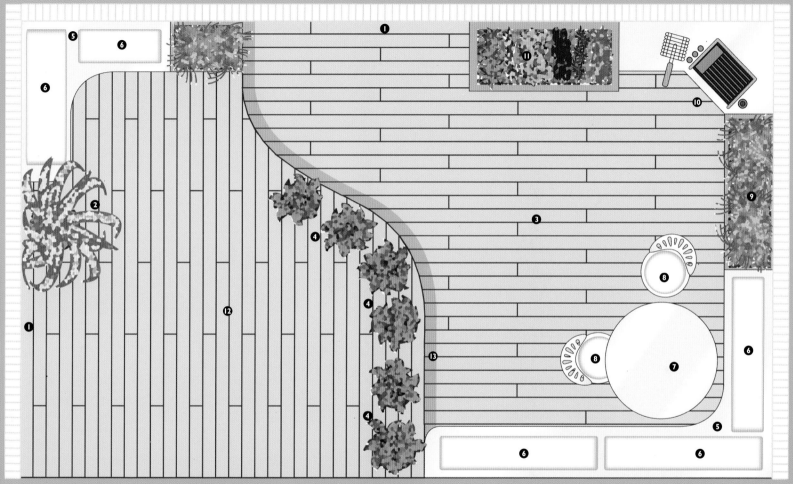

Index

a

acanthus 63
acers 63
alpines 53
angelica 37
annual plants 36
arches 50–1
aspect 13, 16

b

balconies 13, 63
barbecues 32, 70–1
bark chips 30–1, 45, 47, 73
baskets 29, 35
bay trees (*Laurus nobilis*) 63
bedding plants 36, 63, 75
beds 19, 49, 52–3, 56
beech (*Fagus sylvatica*) 42
benches 33, 69
birdbaths 67
bog plants 65
borders 19, 36, 37, 52–3,
    56, 60–1
boundaries 26–9, 38, 42–3
box (*Buxus sempervirens*) 42
bricks 45, 47, 51
buildings 54–5
bulbs 37, 63
busy lizzie (*Impatiens walleriana*) 35

c

cables 22
camomile 49

canary creeper (*Tropaeolum
    peregrinum*) 27
cardoon (*Cynara cardunculus*) 37
castor oil plant (*Ricinus
    communis*) 36
chairs 32–3, 68–9
chic roof garden 100–3
children 15, 31, 48–9, 65, 72–3,
    96–9
choisya 63
clay soil 21
clearing the site 20
clematis 27
climbers 26, 27, 37, 51
climbing frames 72
cobbles 45
cold frames 54–5
colour 28–9, 34–7, 38
containers 34–5, 62–3, 75
Convolvulus tricolor 27
cooking 32, 70–1
cordyline 63
Cosmos bipinnatus 36
Crambe cordifolia 37
creeping thyme (*Thymus
    serpyllum*) 49
crocosmias 37
cup-and-saucer plant (*Cobaea
    scandens*) 27

d

daylilies (*Hemorocallis*) 37
deckchairs 32–3, 69
decking 31, 45

decorative features 37, 66–7
detail 56–76
dining areas 32, 69
dividers 43
drainage 20–1

e

entrances 46, 47

f

family garden 96–9
fences 26–7, 28–9, 43
firethorn (*Pyracantha*) 42
floating plants 65
formal gardens 16–17,60, 64
fountains 64
framework 39–65
furniture 32–3, 68–9

g

gates 46, 47, 56
golden hop (*Humulus lupulus*
    'Aureus') 27, 51
grass 31, 48–9
gravel 30, 31, 45, 47
greenhouses 54, 55

h

hanging baskets 35
hawthorn (*Crataegus
    monogyna*) 42
hedges 42, 43, 75

holly 63
hosta 35, 63
hurdles 27, 43

i

informal gardens 16–17, 60, 64
ivy (*Hedera*) 63

j

jasmine (*Jasminum
    officinale*) 69

l

laurel (*Prunus
    laurocerasus*) 42
lawns 31, 47, 48–9, 56, 72, 74
levelling 13, 20–1
lifestyle 14–15
lighting 67, 69
logs 47
loungers 32–3, 69

m

Macleaya cordata 37
marginal plants 65
mediterranean courtyard 92–5
mind-your-own-business
    (*Soleirolia*) 49
Miscanthus sinensis 37
morning glory (*Ipomoea tricolor*) 27
moss 49
mowing strips 49, 74

n

nasturtium 27
needs 14–15
New Zealand flax (*Phormium tenax*) 35

o

obelisks 50
ornaments 37, 66–7

p

paddling pools 73
paint 28
panel fencing 26–7
pansy (*Viola* x *wittrockiana*) 35
paths 31, 46–7, 49, 50–1
patios 15, 44–5, 56
    barbecues 70
    pergolas 50
    preparation 21
    temporary 30–1
pavers 45
paving slabs 31, 45, 47
pelargonium 35
perennials 36, 37
pergolas 50, 51, 69
pets 15
petunia 35
philadelphus 63
picnic blankets 33
pillars 50
pipes 12–13, 18, 22

planning 18–19, 22, 48
planning permission 43, 55
planting 34–7, 60–1, 65
play equipment 72–3, 76
playhouses 55, 73
pot marigold (*Calendula officinalis*) 35
pots 29, 34–5, 62–3, 67
preparation 20–1
privacy 26–9, 50, 80–3
pyracantha 63

r

railway sleepers 47
raised beds 52–3
reed screens 27, 43
relaxing garden 80–3
Rheum palmatum 37
rock gardens 53, 75
romantic garden 84–7
roof gardens 13, 63, 100–3
roses 75
rotavators 20
rubble 12, 21
runner beans 27, 35

s

safety 15, 31, 65
sand pits 72
screens 26–7, 43
sculptures 67
seating 68–9
services 12–13, 18, 22

setts 45
shade
    borders 52
    instant 33
    lawns 49
    patios 44
    pergolas 50
    planting 61
    seating areas 69
    style 16
    water features 65
sheds 54, 55
slopes 13, 20–1, 65
soil 12, 21, 52, 53, 61
spurge (*Euphorbia characias*) 35
statues 37, 66–7
stepping stones 47
steps 47
style 16–17, 42, 62, 66
summerhouses 54, 55
sun 61, 65
sundials 67
sweet peas (*Lathyrus odoratus*) 27
swings 72–3

t

tables 32
temporary measures 23–38
terraces 13, 20, 44–5, 56
time 14–15, 17, 74–5
tobacco plant (*Nicotiana*) 36, 69
topiary 63
topsoil 12, 21

trees 61, 63
trellis 26, 27, 43
troughs 35, 62, 63
tubs 35

u

urban retreat 88–91
urns 62, 63, 67

v

vertical features 50–1

w

wall pots 29, 35
walls 29, 43
water features 64–5, 76
weedkillers 20
weeds 74–5
willow 51
wind 13
windowboxes 29, 35, 63
wisteria 51
witch hazel (*Hamamelis*) 63
woodstain 28, 43

y

yew (*Taxus baccata*) 42
yucca 35

Acknowledgements

Emap Gardening Picture Library
3 left, 74, /Nick Parish 13.

Garden Picture Library
Brian Carter 18 left, 70, /Eric Crichton 44, 82 bottom right, /Clive Nichols 66, 94 top right, /Lorraine Pullin 54, /Gary Rogers 65, /JS Sira 26, 67, /Georgia Glynn-Smith 94 bottom right, /Juliette Wade 90 top.

John Glove
7 left, 29, /Designer: Chris Jacobson 3 right, 79, /The Malthouse, Gloustershire. 51, /Save the Children/ RHS Chelsea Flower Show 1991 98 top, /Woking Borough Council/ RHS Chelsea Flowers Show 1997 8 bottom.

Octopus Publishing Group Limited
Mark Bolton 38, 48, Cannington College 27, D'arcy & Everest Ltd./ RHS Hampton Court Flower Show 2001 8 top left, Designer Sally Fell/ RHS Hampton Court Flower Show 2001 8 top right, Designer: Christopher Costin/ RHS Hampton Court Flower Show 2001 17, 37 right, 49, Designer: Elizabeth Apedaile/ RHS Hampton Court Flower Show 2001 86 bottom right, Designer: Johnny Woodford & Cleve West/ RHS Chelsea Flower Show 2001 15, Designer: Karen Maskell/ RHS Hampton Court Flower Show 2001 35 right, Designer: Sharon Clarke/ RHS Chelsea Flower Show 2001 3 centre, 62, Hillview Hardy Plants/ RHS Hampton Court Flower Show 2001 7 right, Scots of Thrapston/ RHS Hampton Court Flower Show 2001 35 left, /Peter Pugh-Cook 72, /Rupert Horrox 32 left, /Howard Rice 6, 20, 30, 33, 102 bottom right, /David Sarton/ 'What we Want', The Teenage Garden/ RHS Hampton Court 2002 28 right, Designer: Alan Taylor/ RHS Hampton Court Flower Show 2002 53, Designer: Amanda Broughton/ RHS Hampton Court Flower Show 2002 16, Designer: Cherry Bunton/ RHS Hampton Court Flower Show 2002 52, Designer: Guy Farthing/ RHS Hampton Court Flower Show 2002 94 left, Designer: Hannah Genders Garden Design/ RHS Hampton Court Flower Show 2002 86 top right, Designer: Jane Mooney/ RHS Chelsea Flower Show 2002 47, Designer: Jane Mooney/ RHS Hampton Court Flower Show 2002 28 left, Designer: Keith Clarke & Peter Furze/ RHS Hampton Court Flower Show 2002 64, Designer: Mark Ashmead/ RHS Hampton Court Flower Show 2002 102 bottom left, Designer: Patrick Clarke & Patrick Wynnniatt-Husey/ RHS Chelsea Flower Show 2002 42, Designer: Patrick McCann/ RHS Chelsea Flower Show 2002 61, Designer: Roger Platts/ RHS Chelsea Flower Show 2002 86 left, Designer: Tamsin Woodhouse & Chloe Wood/ RHS Chelsea Flower Show 2002 68, Designers: Mark Walker & Sarah Wigglesworth/ RHS Chelsea Flower Show 2002 31, Orchard Pottery/ RHS Chelsea Flower Show 2002 37 left, Room in a Garden/ RHS Chelsea Flower Show 2002 25, The Bulbeck Foundry/ RHS Chelsea Flower Show 2002 34, /Mel Yates 7 centre.

Jerry Harpur
Designer: Brian Berry 32 right, /Frank Cabot 50, /Designer: Simon Fraser, Middlesex, UK 73, 82 top right, /Designer: Richard Hartlage forGraeme Hardie, NJ, USA 90 bottom right, /Designer: Victor Nelson, NY, USA 90 bottom left, /Designer: Oheme & Van Sweden, USA 82 left, /David Pearson, Highgate, London, UK 102 top left, /Gunilla Pickard 55, /La Roserie, Ouigane, Morocco. 41, /Designer: Mark Rumary, Suffolk, UK. 11.

Marcus Harpur
An Artists Garden/ RHS Chelsea Flower Show 2001 102 top right, /Gerald Brazier, Essex, UK 98 bottom left, /Lakemount Design: Brian Cross, Co.Cork, Ireland 60.

Andrew Lawson
14, 18 right, 59, 63, 75, /Designer: Penelope Hobhouse 19, /Designer: Anthony Noel 12, /Wollerton Old Hall, Shropshire, UK 46.

Clive Nichols
The Abbey House 76, /Garden & Security Lighting 22, /Sarah Leyton 98 bottom right, /Lisette Pleasance 56, /Designer: Elisabeth Woodhouse 36.

Executive Editor Sarah Ford
Editor Camilla James
Executive Art Editor Rozelle Bentheim
Designer Ginny Zeal
Illustrations Bounford.com
Senior Production Controller Ian Paton
Picture Researcher Zoe Holtermann